THE TRUEST THINGS I KNOW

To Darlene!
with love!
Laurel

The Truest Things I Know

5 Simple Lessons for Choosing *Love* over Fear!

LAUREL A. ROSS, PhD

The Truest Things I Know:
5 Simple Lessons for Choosing Love over Fear!

Laurel A. Ross, PhD

ISBN: 978-1-939288-80-6

Library of Congress Control Number: 2014949250

Cover design by Hari Baumbach, PowerUp Productions

Love It! Publishing,
An Imprint of Wyatt-MacKenzie

DEDICATION

To my mother, Carole Anne Lee,
my first teacher of love.

Acknowledgements

As I send this book out into the world, I want to thank all the people who helped me imagine, envision, organize and create it—not to mention the endless editing, polishing and publication of it. My thanks to John Forman, a colleague and friend; Brooke Warner, a publishing coach who appeared at the exact moment I needed her; Nancy Cleary, my imprint Diva who continues to walk me through the potential mine field of publication, and the many friends who read and encouraged me throughout the process.

Finally, and most emphatically, I want to thank my family: Tyler and Dan. My son, Tyler, continues to be a source of inspiration and insight every day. My husband, Dan, who listened to every single chapter, every single word and gave me endless hours of patient and considered feedback. Dan helps me bring more love into the world every moment, just by being in my life.

I am very grateful to you all, and know very well the magic at play in all our lives.

— LAUREL ROSS
VERNON, BRITISH COLUMBIA

TABLE OF CONTENTS

CHAPTER 2

CHAPTER 3

CHAPTER 4

CHAPTER 5

CONCLUSION

Ahh Truth!

*E*ver since I was a little girl I have loved teaching. I drove my friends crazy every summer by holding "school" in my garage. I would collect the extra worksheets from trash cans around my school, and repurpose them into our summer lessons. Of course, I had my favorite subjects; reading and writing were the pillars of my curriculum. I believed that those two disciplines held the secrets to the Universe. I would passionately argue with my friends that one story or another revealed truth—if we could only see through the symbolism. In my lessons, Rapunzel became a treatise for self-discovery and subsequent freedom. Sleeping Beauty became a metaphor for awakening to a happy life. As you might imagine, not many "students" came to my school, but I didn't give up! As I grew older, my passion for story-telling grew with me. I read voraciously. I watched every movie I could lay my hands on. I went into college with one goal in mind: to find more books. Somewhere along the road, I realized that I could combine my love of stories with my love of teaching and my English-teacher Self was born. Through my years as a teacher, I began to notice the same questions percolating through the stories. Year after year, new students would come and go, but the questions remained unchanged. "What is truth?" "Who are we?" "Why are we here?" For twelve years, my students and I explored the answers to those questions down the various roads which our novels, poetry and essays would take us. We all knew there was something more to this game of life than our eyes could tell us, but what, we wondered, was it?

As life would have it, I left teaching literature and writing to create software training at Microsoft, and discovered a whole new world of story-telling. With my background in literature, I was able to see epic themes being played out across the company: heroes and villains, damsels in distress, shining knights in armor coming to save the day. People do love to tell their stories! These stories seemed to have more at stake because they were happening to real people in real lives. Within a few short years, I became a manager and the story-telling became even more obvious and even more intense. I could see the questions I had studied and taught so clearly in my employees' daily lives; Who am I? What is truth? Why are we here? In the process of developing my own leadership skills, I found tools that helped me decode some of these patterns and stories being lived out at work. I started mentoring professional development with my teams and had great success in improving their performance results. Soon, managing one team wasn't enough, and I began mentoring men and women across the company in my "spare" time. I had discovered the power of the story and wanted everyone to know it.

I left Microsoft after nine years to found my own company, Our Imagined Life. As an expert in Training and Development, I built my business on the premise that we hold the keys to our own success and happiness. I noticed my early clients were largely unaware that they had been sabotaging themselves for years. Using my business and teaching experience, I developed a robust set of tools to help my clients explore and shed their own self-defeating stories. As I gained more experience and confidence, I realized that I was actually developing a repeatable process that could work for everyone. I moved away from an exclusive focus on the corporate world to include "regular folks" in my practice. I was delighted to see client after client benefit and grow from recognizing their own self-limiting stories. I discovered my "leadership" tools were really tools for living a happy life. Eight years and more than 350 clients later, my tools have proven to be life-changing: they reveal the truth beneath the stories and to help people realize their dreams.

Now—what does all of this have to do with truth? Along the way I discovered the truest things I know woven through all those stories I told myself and heard from others. From the title of this book you can probably guess that I am not shy about tackling big questions. Who am I? Why am I here? What is truth? If you are like me, perhaps you have been wondering about these questions for most of your life, too. After all, aren't these the questions everyone has been trying to answer for centuries? I haven't always been sure of my own answers. Life had to show me again and again the truth about itself. I had to hear the same stories many times from others before I saw the similarities. "The truth must dazzle gradually," as Emily Dickinson once wrote, and that certainly was true in my case. My entire life has been a process of understanding the truths I have come to know and am about to share with you. My discovery was and continues to be an integration of everything I have ever seen, learned, thought, felt and experienced. In fact, I am still experiencing the day-to-day practice of living my true life. I am a teacher and a practitioner. I have helped many people find their own truth with the simple tools contained in this book. My hope is that these ideas and tools will help you to live the life of your dreams: the life you are truly meant to live.

My Dream of Life

Many years ago, I had a dream that continues to remind me about the nature of my own truth. I dreamed that I was walking on a dirt road. I was in a hurry because it was getting dark. I was alone and the road was rocky. I was afraid of getting lost or hurt in the darkness. As the evening deepened and the road became dim, I grew more and more afraid. I began to hear rustling sounds from the trees and I pictured bad men hiding in the darkness waiting to attack me. I imagined the sound of footsteps behind me on the road. Just when I thought I should find my own place to hide and wait for morning, I stumbled upon an old lantern in the road. As I picked it up, I was surprised to find that it was lit; I could see the light glowing inside, but it was almost completely obscured by the shutters rusted and closed over the glass. Even when I pried open one of the shutters, the glass inside was covered with soot. I spent some time in my dream cleaning off the soot, and working the hinges until I could open and close the shutters smoothly.

When the lantern was clean and the shutters were open, I stood up and lifted the lantern high above my head. I looked around, expecting to see the bad men lurking in the trees, but was amazed to see that I was actually standing in the middle of a beautiful garden. Brightly colored flowers covered the hillsides. The rustling I had heard from the trees in the darkness was the swishing of exotic birds with long, colorful tails. They sat in the trees looking curiously at me. The trail ahead of me was not rocky as I had imagined earlier; it was open and grassy. In the radiant light of my lantern, I could see the extraordinary beauty of that place. I was no longer afraid at all. I felt completely at peace.

I woke up from my dream with two clear thoughts: first, the lantern was already lit when I found it. I did not need a match. It was burning as if it had always been burning. The light inside was radiant. It filled every corner of the darkness in my dream. Second, the light revealed the scene as it truly was, not as the scene my fear had created for me. It showed me that I was standing in a beautiful and peaceful garden. It had always been that way. The darkness was hiding the truth about that garden. In the darkness, I allowed my imagination to run wild. From my perspective of fear, I had created a story about the perils that lurked in the trees waiting to get me. The garden had not changed. My perception of it had changed. The light from my own lantern told me the truth—the truth about the world without my scary story plastered on top of it. I was awake and wondering, "Could the real world be this way, too—this beautiful place of peace and happiness? Was it just a matter of changing my perspective?"

Story-Telling Boot Camp

In my experience, few people realize the power of their own story-telling. Most of us think of a story as an entertainment: something to watch on TV and kick back with after a long day at work. Few of us realize that we live inside our stories all day. It's not our fault, and we're not bad if we do this. We are all a product of the conditioning we undergo as we grow up in this world. I call this conditioning: boot camp. We are born into a well-defined training program with a well-defined system for learning all the "right" things to think, feel and do. All over the world, we operate this boot camp:

a place where we raise our children, as we were raised, steeped in the traditions and stories of our culture. We learn the stories: the stories of what our parents think, what our religious leaders preach, and what our teachers teach. Our stories have grown up with us. For most of us, our stories define our experience and our perception of everything around us. In this boot camp, we also learn how to create our own stories about the whole experience. Boot camp at its best is our collective attempt to live together in harmony. Our parents teach us how to be safe from hot stoves, stay out of dangerous situations and what is required of us to be accepted into society. Unfortunately, some of the stories we learn also teach us to fear and doubt our own logic and reason: our own intelligence. They teach us that we cannot trust ourselves to do the right thing, and that listening to our own hearts is somehow unreliable. Put simply, our conditioning in Boot Camp doesn't prepare us for what is really true about life. We leave it, as we leave childhood, with our attention focused on of the *stories* of our experience rather than on the *truths* which underlie them.

For most of my life, I believed that I was the "lesser sister." I lived in the shadow of my sister's glory. She was everything I was not—or so the story went. She was beautiful; I was only cute. She was super smart; I was smart enough. She was slim; I was curvy. On and on and on, the story goes. It wasn't her fault that my parents told us that story; in fact, it wasn't my parents' fault either. They both came from competitive families and were taught that comparisons created healthy competition and the desire to improve. Their story was the result of the Boot Camp into which both my parents were born. Though they did not intend that training to harm me, the story defined my view of myself. I spent years believing and living the story of the lesser sister. I achieved various successes, but never more than my sister. Believing that the story was true, I maintained my role in the story. I held myself back—not deliberately, but my belief of being the "lesser sister" manifested itself, nonetheless. Fortunately, in my adult years I was able to identify my story about my sister, dislodge it from my sense of the "truth" about it and see myself as I truly was: a talented, well-educated, beautiful, curvy woman. I had my gifts, and my sister had hers. I also discovered that she had her own stories about her deficiencies. We decided to write a new story together built around the closeness and love we truly felt for each other rather than the competition my parents' story had imposed on us.

See Your Stories

Are you noticing a story of you own right now? Are you "the lesser" sibling or partner on the team at work? Do you find yourself wondering about what stories you might be telling yourself that keep you locked in a box of self-limitation? Are you curious about how you may be holding yourself back, caught in an unconscious story of your own? In order to take a look at your stories, let's walk through a visualization I use with my clients to help them identify some of those stories.

Imagine you are sitting in an empty movie theatre. You are relaxed and peaceful in your seat, waiting for the movie to start. The lights go down, but instead of seeing one movie on the large screen, you begin to see many, smaller movies scattered across the screen like individual pictures. Each of the movies is a different story from your life. You can see one of you as a child and another one of you learning to swim, or ride a bicycle. Perhaps another story begins on the opposite side of your screen showing you pictures of your school days: elementary school, junior high school, high school, etc. Story after story lights up in front of you as you trace the events of your whole life: some happy and some sad, some painful and some filled with joy. Now the stories focus on your present life. Can you see them?

Perhaps they are stories of your relationships or challenges you are having at work. Perhaps they are stories of longing, yearning for something more. These are the stories of your life flashing in front of you in a beautiful mosaic of your experiences: successes, failures, mistakes and triumphs. These are the stories that help you to make sense of your world. Whenever you encounter a new situation, you automatically refer to your stories to understand it. Which ones catch your attention in this moment? What do you find yourself noticing about those pictures, now?

Now imagine that the screen floats down off the wall, bringing your stories with it and surrounds you in a kind of viewing capsule. You are still sitting comfortably in your seat, but the screen has surrounded you. Now that the screen is closer to you, you realize it is transparent—like glass—and the stories and pictures are MUCH clearer—like having your own personal high-definition viewing screen. In fact, if I hadn't told you that you were looking through a screen, you might never have noticed the transparent overlay of your stories. You can watch your life stories all the time. You can summon them as quickly as you can form a thought. You have thousands of experiences, lessons you have learned and expertise about the world that you can call on at any given moment to help you decide what everything means on the other side of the screen. The stories show you how to behave, what to think and how to feel. This is the catalogue of your experience with this thing called life, you gather more stories about yourself and your world until your view screen becomes crowded with images. It would be impossible to see all the stories unless you had found a way to group them around certain categories: love, fear, relationships, parenting, work, money, success, death, God. Can you see some of those stories? Do you notice any categories you have created? You probably have an elaborate sorting system for your view screen which is created from years of experience: of knowing what works and what doesn't and it is probably completely invisible to you. That is, you are unaware of it—until now. Part of your sorting system comes from internal, individual insights and part of it comes from external influences. Whatever sorting mechanism you use, you always have ready access to your stories to help you make sense of your experience and your world. I have a sorting system of my own which I use through this book. You will want to keep your stories in mind as you read. We will be referring to your stories as a way of seeing and seeing beyond them to something truer.

Story-Telling 101

Your HD viewing capsule is like a mission control center. You sit comfortably in your chair surrounded by pictures of your life, and you are in control. You have the "Con"—as they say in the military. You control the stories—or do you? While it is true that you are able to summon your stories at will, they may also appear when you are not conscious of them. Remember: your view screen is transparent. Some of your stories are programmed to automatically pop up when triggered by events, emotions and other people. Try answering the question "who am I?" What pictures begin popping up on your screen? What stories rev up in response? "Who am I?" Pictures of the roles you play or the work you do may fill your screen: you may see yourself as a mother or father, as a child, as an employee, a friend or a lover. Your pictures and your stories tell you all of these things, but are they the truest answer? Is there more to you than the stories tell you?

In order to answer those questions, you must become aware of two things: first, you are not your story. You are the one watching the story. If you can shift your attention out of the stories on your view screen, you are clearly NOT the story itself. You are sitting in the position of observation. Now, focus your attention on yourself as the one watching the view screen. You may be the main character in the story you are watching, but you are only a character. You can see the other characters in the story, too. You are not those characters, either. As the observer sitting in the chair, you can call yourself back to center, out of the story and return to being the observer in the chair, at any moment. Can you place your attention on the Observer watching the screen right now? Can you become the observer reading this book, for example? For most of my clients, this is an all-important first step: to notice where they are placing their attention. Now that you are in the position of the observer, what quality of experience does the observer have? The observer has awareness: awareness of you sitting in the chair as well as the awareness of the story being projected on the view screen. Now, you could say that you have moved beyond being the observer to become the Awareness. You are the Awareness sitting in the chair.

Now that you are the Awareness, the second thing to notice about your story is that the story you are watching is only partially true. The story seems true; it feels true. In fact, it is probably based on real events that happened to you, or that you actually observed. I fell off my bicycle and hit my head really hard when I was 10 years old. That really happened! But, did that one incident define my truth about bicycles? Are all bicycles dangerous and suspect now? Of course not! While it is true that I had a dangerous accident on my bicycle, it is not the whole truth about bicycles. Nor is it the whole truth about my other experiences with bicycles. Our stories are true—but only partially true—and that is the limit of story-telling. The stories are bound by perspective. They are chronicles of our experience, our conditioning and our frame of reference. We run into trouble when we forget that simple fact. Our stories keep us inside our viewing capsule, in a prison of our own perspective. The picture you saw when you asked the question "Who am I?" only partially reflected all that is true about you. All those roles you play, even the awareness you may have of yourself as an individual, is not the whole truth of who you are.

You Are Not Alone

What happens to your viewing capsule when you go out into the world? It is simple enough to picture this mission control center when you are alone, but how does it change as you enter the world? The answer is: it doesn't. In fact, you take your stories with you wherever you go—but don't worry! You are not alone. Everyone else has their stories, too. Like you, they have their view screens and their stories. They went through Boot Camp, too. In fact, everyone in your neighborhood, town, city, state, nation, and country has their view screen running. In a way, it is comforting to know that we all face the same challenge of separating ourselves from our stories. Have you ever met someone, or tried to talk to someone and felt like you were talking to a brick wall? It is possible that you were talking to their story. It is really hard to talk to someone who is lost in their story. They are insulated behind a thick wall of their own experience, and it is almost impossible to break through. In many ways, you are invisible to them. You are just a character in their story.

Have you ever noticed that you tell many of the same stories as your friends or family? This is called collective story-telling: a story that has been told so many times and by so many people that we all believe it is true. In the 1950's most women believed that being a mother was the highest calling they could answer. It was a collective story that defined many women's goals and choices. It may or may not have been the truest or best path for the individual, but it was a collective story for women. We have collective stories about many of the roles we play: a mother, or father, a boyfriend or girlfriend, a citizen of a certain country, or member of a religion, or political affiliation, even the laws of the land are collective stories we agree to tell and re-tell. All of these collective stories give us information about how to live successfully in a society. It is comforting to find stories that match our own, and it is completely understandable that we would want such comfort. We want to fit in, and belong to a community. That is a natural human urge. Finding our common stories is one of the ways we do this. We use our stories, individually and collectively, to make sense of the world around us, even when those stories do not reflect who we truly are.

Most people experience the relationship with their stories as one of cause and effect: the story is the cause and their life is the effect. That story you might be telling yourself about how you can never get what you want is causing you the pain of never achieving your goals. The story you tell yourself about not having enough money creates a permanent feeling of scarcity which defines most of your actions around money. Those stories you tell yourself about being over-weight, having no friends, failing in relationships or being undeserving, define the life you are living. To interrupt the cause and effect relationship between the story and your life, you must separate yourself from your story. You must see your story AS a story. It is easy to understand why we think we ARE the story. We all have an impressive collection of experiences and we believe those experiences must define who we are—right? Who are you if not the main character in this "life" you are seeing on your screen?

Who Are You?

When you can see yourself as the Awareness inside the screen, you can also see beyond your stories. The stories become objects, things you can watch. The stories may reflect true and accurate events that have happened in your life, but those stories do not automatically tell you the truth about who you are—only what has happened to you. The truth is that you are the Awareness. You are the one bringing your attention to the stories inside the screen. What is the Awareness? The awareness is your connection to the Divine. It is your connection to your innate, spiritual essence. It is powered by the Divine: the radiant, loving energy that is ever-present, and unchanging. It sits in stark contrast to the stories you see projected on your view screen. The stories are the chronicle of your human experience, but they are not you. You are the embodiment of Spirit and the awareness inside the screen is your Truest Self.

Try this: let your view screen go blank. Let the stories you have been watching stop. Story by story let your screen go quiet. Take a deep breath, relax your mind and turn off the screen; sit in a quiet capsule. If you cannot turn off the stories, perhaps you can mute them, so that all you see is the flashing light on the screen without sound. Let the silence sink into your bones and fill you with the radiant energy of the Divine. You are the Awareness; you are a radiant being of light; you hold that light in your physical form. Without the stories to distract you, what thoughts occur to you now? What can you see as you look through your empty screen to the world beyond? The world becomes a very different place when we have the courage to stop seeing it through our stories.

Who Are We?

I began to discover the truest things I know as I practiced turning off my stories and looking out from behind my view screen. I saw simple truths behind the stories. In fact, the stories held valuable pointers to a larger truth. Those truths point to the BIG truth: that we are all spiritual beings. We come from a loving source, carry love with us into this world, and, if we are true to our calling, we create more love in the world. I know it is hard to believe this truth when we look out to a world full of fear, anger and hatred, violence and poverty, but all the other true things I will discuss are built on this greatest truth. That guy on the freeway driving too fast is a spiritual being. The woman who took cuts in line at the store is a spiritual being. Our beloved family and friends are spiritual beings. Why is the world in such a terrible mess, if we are all spiritual beings? We seem to have forgotten who we are. We are born into the world of the physical and we grow up in Boot Camp forgetting our True Selves. We are conditioned to fear rather than to love. We are conditioned to doubt ourselves rather than to embrace our inner awareness and wisdom.

Don't blame yourself if you have forgotten your own spiritual nature, or lost track of it along your way. Most of my clients come to me in that same state. You were born onto the planet of forgetfulness, processed through a systematic Boot Camp experience, raised by parents who may have also forgotten their Truest Selves into a society that celebrates and reinforces the numb, forgetfulness of the world. You may have heard this for-getfulness likened to being asleep; I prefer to think of it as having forgotten something that we knew was true. Perhaps that yearning is what drove you to pick up this book. That deep sense of yearning that most of us feel, that quiet longing for something more, is the evidence of trying to remember the truth: that we are spiritual beings created for self-determination into a world of infinite possibilities of experience. What keeps us wrapped in our forgetful fog? Why is it so hard to integrate our spiritual nature with our physical life? We will answer these questions and many more in the pages of this book.

"There" is Here

Would it surprise you to know that there is no journey to enlightenment? What if I told you that you are already there? This is not a journey and there is no destination. You are the Awareness sitting in the chair. In one breath, you can focus your attention on your own Awareness and "arrive" at your destination. You already exist as a spiritual being. You have always been a spiritual being. The yearning you feel—that yearning for something more—is evidence of your spiritual nature. It is your spiritual essence calling to you. Now, you are also experiencing what it is like to have a human body in a physical world. Part of that physical experience means aligning your awareness, your True Self with your actions and behaviors. This is not an exploration of how to be more spiritual; you are already a spiritual being. This is a book about how to be truly human, to cherish the human experience you are having as a spiritual being, and to bring all of your loving energy and intention into the world.

Life Beyond the Story

What kind of life are you living now? Are you cherishing yourself? Do you feel abundant and joyful? Do you experience the miracle of your true life every day? What kind of life might be possible if you could turn off your view screen with all its story-telling and live each moment with the awareness of your Truest, Divine Self? That world is quite different from the world you see through your screen. It is already out there—waiting to be discovered. Is that something that interests you? In the course of the book, we will talk about fear. We will put fear in its place and find ways to keep it from defining our life. We will loosen the grip of scarcity that has most of us planning worst-case scenarios. We will talk about the self-doubt, and the stories of giving up, growing tired and letting our dreams fade. We will talk about the mistakes we've made, and the lessons we've learned. We will let ourselves admit that money scares the hell out of most us, and why it does. We will even talk about the scariest thing of all—death. All these stories have truth in them, and look quite different when told without the distraction of your view screen. Perhaps every once in a while, as your personal stories grow quiet, you have had the sense of something more, something beyond the stories you tell yourself. "Is this all there is?" you ask yourself. Of course you would ask—you are a spiritual being having an earthly experience, and your spirit longs to re-connect with the truth beyond the screen. We all yearn to live in alignment with our deepest truth. A part of you already knows what that truth actually is and finding it for yourself is the greatest gift you will ever give yourself and the world.

It's Your Choice!

For many years, I have been working with men and women helping them to investigate their stories and change their lives to live happier, more authentic lives. Client after client has come to me, needing tools to sort through the stories they had created for themselves. Self-made prisoners of their own perspective, they sat inside their viewing screens, unaware that they were watching their self-limiting stories and trying to make sense of a world through a filter of their past. They all had so many things in common, so many similar stories and themes that I began to notice patterns in the ways in which they kept themselves distracted from the truth. Even working with large corporations and groups, I saw the same unmistakable "truths" emerging. I decided to write this book in the hopes of reminding everyone of the simple truths about our experience here that many people have forgotten, or perhaps never knew. I might have been content to stay in my smaller circle, helping people one at a time if not for the fact that we are approaching a tipping point in the world today. We must act, and act in alignment with the truth of our essential nature. We can do more; we can change the world and bring our dreams to life. We must focus our attention away from the damaging story-telling that keeps us all locked in our prisons of perspective, and bring more of our true, loving nature into the world. Do you want to continue to watch your view screen? Do you want to live your life collecting stories about your experience, or would you rather find out what is happening behind the screen? Would it be exciting or frightening (or both)? Would it be helpful to know what truth lives in all the stories you tell yourself? How might it change your life to know that? How might our world be different if we all lived in alignment with our Divine, Truest Selves?

As I mentioned earlier, each of the chapters is

designed to help you look at your stories more directly in order to find the truths which are hidden underneath. I chose the majors themes I have discovered in the course of my work: fear, scarcity, honesty, death and responsibility. My hope is that in telling you these stories and the truth that I found hidden in them you will be able to do the same—to look at the world and at yourself, not with the judgment and limitation of your view screen, but with complete love and acceptance. My hope is to show you how to open the shutters of your own lantern, and shine your light more brightly into the world. My hope is that by telling you the truest things *I* know, you will begin to be curious about the truest things *you* know. That is the beginning of a wonderful adventure, and who knows where that will take us if we travel together. I suspect that as we all begin to admit the truest things we know to ourselves and others we will find the world changing beneath our feet in ways we can only imagine. It is time to remember who you truly are, and bring your Truest Self into the world!

CHAPTER 1

There's Nothing Under the Bed

(and that's why it's scary)

"I have it in me, so much nearer home—to scare myself with my own desert places."

ROBERT FROST

It was 3 o'clock in the morning. I was 4 years old: awake and terrified. The room was dark and shadowy. I could hear my sister, Julie, in the bunk above me breathing quietly and knew she was sound asleep. My brother David, across the room in his twin bed, was also asleep. I needed to go to the bathroom, but I fully believed that a monster, lurking under my bed, would grab my ankles just as my feet hit the floor. The very thought of it had me gripped in fear, unable to move. I calculated how far I would have to jump to be far away enough from the monster's reach, but I didn't have the confidence to try it. If I missed my mark, the consequences would be too dire. The monster would get me!

I whispered as loudly as I dared to my sister in the bunk above. Above all, I didn't want to wake up the monster under the bed, too; I just wanted to get Julie's protection to walk me to the bathroom. Finally, I woke her up, and somewhat begrudgingly she walked me down the short hall to the bathroom and waited to walk me back. This was our nighttime ritual. I don't know how many nights we went through our little drama, but finally Julie had had enough and told my mother that I was afraid of the monster under my bed. My mother's reaction surprised me. She wasn't upset or angry. In fact, she wasn't even afraid. She went right into our bedroom and looked under the bed. I followed her, knowing she would see nothing. It was daylight, and the monster was never there during the day. She asked me to tell her about the monster, so I told her all about the horrible scary "thing" under my bed. I told her about how afraid I was that some night he might change his mind about grabbing me only when I got out of bed, and actually grab me while I was still in my bed. She asked me to describe what he looked like. Though I had never actually seen his face, I knew EXACTLY what he looked like. I described him with such detail even my mother had to admit that he sounded very scary! He was not an animal and not a man. He was a dark, shadowy creature that lived in the dust and the darkness of unused places. He hid in the shadows waiting to grab little girls on their way to the bathroom.

That night, my mother tucked me into bed as usual, but instead of leaving the room, she sat at the foot of the bed and told me she had a plan. I couldn't imagine what she was talking about, so that familiar wave of fear started building in my gut. Then she pulled out a shiny silver flashlight. She said that she wanted to conduct a scientific experiment. "Let's turn off all the lights, and see what will happen if we shine a flashlight under the bed." Well, that didn't sound very smart to me. We had done other scientific experiments that involved the chemistry of making cookies or the botany of planting flowers, but investigating the shadowy reaches under my bed with a flashlight didn't sound like science to me. My mother proceeded to turn off the lights, and come back to the foot of my bed.

We sat together in the darkness for a few minutes, and then my mother asked me what I could see. I could see the bunk bed. I could see my mother sitting there. I could even see across the room to my brother's bed.

Then she handed me the flashlight and said, "Whenever you're ready, go ahead and turn on the flashlight and look under the bed." I'm not sure how long it took me to gather my courage, but of course, it seemed like an eternity. Finally, I clicked on the flashlight. I shone it on my mother's face, and she smiled at me, then I leaned over the edge of the bed, and moved the beam of light around to see what I could see. I saw the hardwood floors and the dust and far off in the corner a missing Scrabble letter—no monster and no sign of a monster. I got out of bed and hunkered down on the floor for a better look, an extremely brave move, I thought, given that a few minutes earlier I was sure I would see some gaping mouth ready to bite me! I looked as far around the room from the floor as my flashlight would show me. I saw lots of dust, and when I mentioned that to my mother she chuckled, saying "Yes, we'd better use the dust mop tomorrow, don't you think?" I climbed back into bed, ready to discuss the whole scientific experiment.

"Mom," I asked her. "Where did the monster go?" I still had lurking suspicions that he might come back. My mother smiled again and said, "There's nothing under the bed, Laurel, and that's why it is scary. You see, you have a great imagination, and you are imagining something much scarier than could ever be there. The monster won't come back, because now you know what is REALLY under the bed—your imagination. Why not picture flowers, instead?" She gave me kisses and cuddles and left me in the dark room, no longer afraid. I fell right to sleep, and when I woke up later that night, I grabbed my shiny silver flashlight and pointed it under the bed. I saw the dust, the missing Scrabble letter, and the empty spaces in between. I climbed out of bed without fear, went to the bathroom all by myself, and tucked myself back in without waking up my sister. I even took a few minutes to shine my flashlight around the room, and I remember thinking how interesting the room looked in the darkness, and how different things looked in the beam of the flashlight. I fell back to sleep feeling happy and peaceful, picturing flowers under my bed.

The Monster Under Your Bed

What role does fear play in your life? What is your monster under the bed? Fear is one of those stories we all have in common. Many of us have the same fear stories with the same characters, plots and outcomes. The view screens you saw in the Introduction gave you a sense of how quickly your stories can rev up and multiply. Fear stories are especially nasty, and tough to examine. It may comfort you to know that you are not alone in your fears. In fact, a recent Gallop poll identified the top ten fears around the world and proved that we all share the same fears. Some of us fear failure. Some of us fear loneliness almost as much as we fear intimacy. Others of us fear being taken advantage of or losing control. According to Gallop, everyone fears death. Let's face it, some of us fear EVERYTHING! Is fear fundamentally a part of our human experience? Is it something we can ever shed? It seems to be a requirement of having a physical body that we fear the physical world. We learned as children that when we fall down—it hurts! We learned that we can scrape our knees, break bones and bleed. These early experiences with pain train us to fear for our physical safety.

As we grow up, our fears grow with us. The monster under our bed becomes a chasm of infinite terror. We replace our concern for a scraped knee with larger and more painful fears: fears of loss, hardship, ruin and death. We learn that when we do something that our parents don't like we are punished—that hurts, too! We are disciplined in a variety of ways which are not always gentle. It is perfectly natural to learn to fear these things. As our view of the world expands, so does our list of things we can fear, and the truth is those things are real. People do lose their jobs. People do live on the streets.

People fail, and hurt and suffer all around the world every day. It is a reality of life. One could argue that the very nature of living is fear. But, before we run out and throw ourselves off a cliff in despair, let us at least ask the question: how shall we respond to the reality that fear exists? How shall we reconcile knowing that pain surrounds our physical body with the truth that we are more than a physical body? If we accept the premise that we are all spiritual beings having this physical experience, how can we uncouple our fear from that experience? Like two train cars hooked to each other, we can disconnect the fear from our experience of this life. We can learn new ways to interact with our own fear. In other words, how do we live a life that is not defined by fear? It would be perfectly understandable to do so: to live our lives in the sequestered safety of our homes. Yet, something pulls us onward and out of our fear. Something whispers in the back of our minds— there is more to life than this. Perhaps, we wonder, "are my fears even real?" Life is miraculous and far more expansive than our fears would ever allow us to believe. Fear could not possibly define the miracle we live every day. Fear must be an unreliable echo from the darkness and shadow we want to leave behind.

Step back from the edge of your fear for a moment. Step back to a quieter place inside yourself. Turn off the stories you have revved up as you read these pages. Remember you are the Awareness in the chair. Let me sit quietly on the foot of your bed as you tell yourself about the monster that lurks underneath. Let me offer you a flashlight to investigate the truth of those fearful stories. Together, let us find the power of reframing your fear, so that you can find flowers under your need instead of monsters, and live a life full of joy and happiness.

Looking Under the Bed

Before you can practice a new way to see your fear, you need to identify a fear plaguing you. Let yourself take a peek under that bed. Like most of the people I work with, you are probably keenly aware of a fear that troubles you. You don't need too much prompting to immediately know what you fear. If you are feeling overwhelmed, then choose something small. That will work, too. Sometimes it is helpful to choose something that nags at you rather than something that terrifies you. Can you hear it nagging? Now think about all the details surrounding that fear. Maybe you are wishing you could change your career, or tell your mother to stop some behavior that bothers you. Maybe you are afraid to tell anyone what you really want. Maybe you are afraid that you don't even know what you want! Perhaps you are afraid you will never have any friends, or that no one will ever understand you. Perhaps you are afraid that you are not worthy or deserving of friendships, at all.

Now imagine that your fear starts up your storytelling and fills your viewing screen with all sorts of pictures telling you that you will never escape your fear. You try and try, but you cannot be successful. It is just too hard. When fear is telling the story, it can only tell you scary things. It is an emotion. It is not reality. The fear of failure, for example, may include actually achieving your goal, but suffering some unnamed consequence as a result. Your fear of never having any friends or of being tragically misunderstood may begin with having friends and losing them if you don't flatter and fawn. Your fear of death may be visited on your children, and you show yourself pictures and stories about that atrocity. Whatever the story, your fear is writing the story that will keep you from living a happy life and achieving your dreams. The fear story is scaring the best out of you!

Fear is only the first stop of this self-defeating storytelling. Psychology 101 teaches us that most of our more negative emotions are secondary to fear. That is, fear comes first and then goes underground into other emotions like anger, cynicism, and despair. If you find yourself feeling angry, you may want to wonder if you are afraid of something. Fear is the first stop, anger is the second. Look at a mother yelling angrily at her child who just ran across the street. The mother is angry because she is afraid that her child may have gotten hurt. When fear becomes exhausting, we morph our fears into secondary emotions. After all, fear can only take you so far. It tends to leave you paralyzed and motionless. The mother fearing for her child's safety cannot act to save her child if she is paralyzed in her fear. Her anger pushes her into action—actual movement against her fear. After repeated cycles of fear into anger, we begin to grow cynical. "I've been down this road before," we say to ourselves, and it was never truer. After a lifetime of being angry with unresolved fears, we adopt the cynical view that things will never change. We accept our "lot" in life, and the fear at the base of it all—wins! These emotions are all the hand-maidens of fear. Check yourself for these stories, and wonder what you fear underneath them.

Fear as a Roadmap

Here is an example of one set of fears I helped a former client of mine conquer. It can function as a kind of roadmap through fear. This was her process of look-ing under her bed, and naming one of her monsters. It was a life-long fear she had, and one that had grown and collected others around it and in support of it. It serves as an excellent example of the kind of nested story-telling we can engage in when fear is in control.

A year or so ago I met a woman, Marion, at one of my presentations. I was talking about living our dreams, and she was inspired by the message and scheduled a private session with me. She came to see me hoping I could help her to lose weight, so that she would feel better about running for the School Board in her district. I had helped other clients with weight-loss before so it didn't seem to be an impossible goal to me. In fact, losing weight is pretty straight forward. Marion was in her 50's and had been trying to shed 75 pounds for her entire adult life. She was afraid that she would be over-weight forever—that she could NEVER lose the 75 extra pounds she had been carrying for the past 30 years. We talked about all the ways she had tried to lose weight before without success. She told me that she had tried everything, but she always gained the weight back, or didn't lose enough to make any real difference. 75 extra pounds is a heavy weight to carry both physically and emotionally, and she was sick of it. We talked about her fears, and I suggested to her that the monster under her bed had many faces; faces she had created down through the years of unsuccessful dieting. We needed to look at all of them. I pointed out to her that she had successfully lost weight in the past, but hadn't been able to keep it off. This time would be different because we would deal with all her fears together.

Marion's list of fears looked like this:

She was afraid of the scale.

She was afraid to weigh herself every day.

She was afraid she would be hungry.

She was afraid she wouldn't like the food she could eat.

She was afraid she would eat the wrong thing, and of course,

She was afraid she wouldn't lose any weight.

She was afraid she would gain any weight back that she had lost.

She was afraid that she would be fat for her entire life.

She was afraid she couldn't get elected to the School Board weighing so much.

In fact, almost everything about her weight loss program scared her, but we forged ahead, exchanging emails, having regular appointments, and keeping her fears out in the open. As she began to lose weight, more fears surfaced. She realized that her family had taught her how to eat her own fears. The old saying, "it's not what you eat; it's what is eating you" was never more true than in her family. She ate to quell all her fears, and her fears were a feast! As Marion learned new ways to deal with her fear directly, her weight continued to come off.

We used Marion's list of fears as a roadmap to her success. We dismantled her fears and used them to tell us specifically how she could succeed in her weight loss. In doing so, they changed from fear into success. We made her fears a problem-solving list, using it to target the things she felt worried or bothered by. Her fear of weighing every day, for example, became a game she could play with her scale: she weighed herself on days when she knew she had "cheated," and took the day off weighing when she had stayed on her program. She found that by using her own fear of the scale as a motivator, she was far more likely to stay on her program as a way of avoiding the scale. She weighed once a week with me, and had the thrill of seeing bigger weight loss numbers on a *weekly* basis than she would have seen on a *daily* basis. Her fear of eating the wrong thing when she went out inspired her to make a list of safe foods: everything that she could eat. Her fear of being hungry translated into having more frequent mini-meals, and allowing herself to eat every time she felt hungry. She discovered that she was much happier "grazing" than in having larger meals. These are solutions that weight-loss systems have been making for years, but the point is that Marion needed to use them as a way of addressing her fears. They may seem like small changes to make, but they were powerful when applied to soothing her fears.

Now, Marion has lost 80 pounds since the day she first came to see me. She was successful in her run for the School Board, and is working on addressing her new fears of being a part of that governing body. You see, the fear doesn't go away for most of us. Though we may wish we could lose our fears forever, most of us just become better at managing it, and learning from it. In some cases, it may be helpful to keep your fear as an advisor. Marion didn't eliminate all her fear; she observed it. Instead of her fear driving her decision-making, her fear became a kind of consultant to her goals. She listened and made changes to her program as necessary, and stayed on track with her desire to lose weight. What can we learn from this about the nature of fear?

Put Fear in its Place

You put fear in its place when you dismantle the fear and look for the part of it that can become a solution, rather than a problem. Dismantling and reframing is the process of shifting your attention from your fear to your ability to change a situation or condition which is fearful to you. When fear is telling the story, everything looks impossible. But, fear does not belong in a position of authorship, because it never tells a happy story. In fact, it lies. It tells you a story of defeat, pain and suffering, and as you watch that story on your view screen you allow yourself to believe it. Fear cannot give you the truth; it can only tell you that something has triggered the warning system for your safety. Confucius once said "you cannot carve rotten wood," and fear is the rotten wood of your mind. If you want to live a life based on clear thinking and conscious choices, then turn off the fear stories. Fear can only give you emotional information about what is going on inside your own mind; it can never tell you about the reality of any situation. Even when you are staring down the barrel of a gun, fear is not the best decision-maker. Fear can tell you that you feel threatened, but it cannot tell you what the best course of action might be. Fear can only tell you that you are reacting to something. It might be inside you or outside you, but it is only an emotion. When you turn off your fear story, you allow your Awareness to examine the fear, to be curious about it. When you stop letting fear make your decisions for you, you make room in your own mind for other information to pour in. You can customize your own success by listening to and honoring your fears. Your fear is telling you how to succeed, if you decode its messages by observing it rather than feeling it.

When you put fear in its place, you allow the churning, muddy water of your emotion to settle into clarity. You create space around it, into which something else can flow. That something else is quiet. It is peaceful. It has a kind of relaxation and release associated with it. It is like taking a deep breath and setting the fear inside a glass box in front of you. Now you have space; now you have the freedom to examine the fear, to question it. Now you can become curious about the fear.

Question Your Fear

Fear arises in us through layers of our experience. Like Maslow's Hierarchy of Needs, each level of our development is driven by new fears. Just as you added more fears to your story-telling, each new level of your own personal growth and development adds more energy to your fear engine. Our lower levels of fear demand our physical safety and security. Ask yourself: "Am I in real danger?" Once you have eliminated that base fear, however, you give yourself much more space and time to examine and analyze your fear. If you are confronted with an agitated rattlesnake, for example, that is not the time to engage in a lengthy analysis of your personal safety. That is the time for action—get out of the way! Fortunately, most of us enjoy physical safety, and our fears are more internally derived. Those are the fears we can question. You can ask yourself: what information is this fear giving me about the present situation? What is it telling me about myself? Why am I afraid right now? Is there anything I can do about this fear? —or is this just another monster under my bed? Depending on the fear you are feeling these questions may change and others will occur to you, but the point is to be curious about your fear. Instead of fearing it, question it.

I had the opportunity to question my own fears on the frightening and terrible day the doctors told my sister, Julie, that she had breast cancer. I was her support system as she navigated those treacherous waters, and I discovered that I had to learn to keep my own fear at bay during doctor's appointments and consultations.

After her first surgery, the doctors brought us into the examination room and told Julie that she had one of the most virulent forms of breast cancer, and that they had not been able to get "clean margins." It meant she would have to undergo chemotherapy, radiation and the possibility of more surgery. It meant that my 38-year-old sister was fighting for her life. As we left the doctor's office that day, Julie told me, "Now I understand one of the ways that cancer kills people. It scares them to death." I have always remembered that and used it to interact with my own fear rather than succumb to it. We can scare ourselves to death with big, scary ideas, and big, scary problems, if we allow our fears to define us. You are not your fear. No matter how big it is, or how scary it is, no matter how real or false it is, you don't have to let it rule your behavior. You can shift your attention to your Awareness of your fear. You can see it, listen to it and acknowledge the information it gives you, and return to your goal. You can integrate the information your fear gave you as necessary and appropriate. The problems may be quite real, but in clinging to your fear of the problem, you limit the possibilities you might otherwise see for solving it by keeping the space of the observer around it. If you keep fear in its place, your fear can become a source of information about your own personal transformation.

Tool: **Dialogue with your Fear**

Let me show you a skill I learned from Ira Progoff's Dialogue Journal technique many years ago, and have adapted it into a tool for using your Awareness to observe your fear. I will use my fear of Julie's fight with breast cancer to demonstrate that even big fears can still be observed. I will engage in a written conversation—a dialogue—with my fear. You can try this on your own after you see the technique. Take a slow, deep breath!

Begin by naming your fear:

Example: My fear is that I will lose my sister, Julie, to breast cancer.

Write a focusing statement as if YOU are the fear:

I am Laurel's fear. I became real when Laurel heard the doctor telling Julie that she had a very dangerous form of breast cancer which had already metastasized into her lymph nodes. I am huge. I am cold and real. I live inside Laurel's heart and mind all the time, now. I want her to notice me.

Engage in a conversation with the fear by asking a question and listening for the answer. I have provided some basic questions to help you begin but please feel free to follow your own instincts on this exercise. Your fear may have other things to tell you about it, so be prepared to listen and interact as your fear directs.

Trust the process, because if you sit quietly, you will hear answers. Write what you hear, even if it doesn't make any sense at first. You are practicing a new skill, so be patient with yourself. Perfection is not necessary. Just ask the following questions, and listen for the answers.

January 1994: I am afraid of losing my sister, Julie, to breast cancer.

Laurel: What is my fear?

Fear: *I am Laurel's fear of losing Julie to breast cancer.*

Laurel: What other fears are joined to this one?

Fear: *Laurel fears the pain of losing her loved one. Laurel fears the sadness the whole family will feel. Laurel fears for her son losing his aunt.*

Laurel fears having no best friend like Julie ever again.

Laurel fears being left behind.

Laurel: Will these fears come true? Will they happen?

Fear: *I am real, but I don't know the future.*

Laurel: Why am I so afraid to look at you?

Fear: *I am fear! I won't go away just because you don't want to look at me. You will still know I am here.*

Laurel: What do you want from me?

Fear: *I want your fear! I want you to know that something bad is happening!*

Laurel: Is there anything else you want me to know?

Fear: *I want you to know that you have to pay attention to me and stop pretending I am not here. I will scream and scream at you until you listen. I want you to know that you will not be able to pay attention to anything else that is going on if you don't pay attention to me.*

Laurel: Since you won't go away, is there anything I can do to make you feel better?

Fear: *This helps. I seem to be relaxing a bit by just having you pay attention to me. Do you feel that, too?*

Laurel: Yes, please give me specific actions to take when you are very strong in me.

Fear: *1. You can pay attention to me every day. 2. You can write about me every day. 3. You can listen to the details of my fear, and if possible change the situation to ease it.*

Laurel: If I do these things, would that help you feel better?

Fear: *Yes, I think it would. As long as you don't*

pretend I'm not real. I think that would work.

Laurel: Is there anything else you want me to know?

Fear: *No. I think that is all I have to say right now.*

End your dialogue with fear with the following statement:

Thank you for the information and insights you have given me. I promise I will continue to use this information in a healthy way for my own growth and development. I am at peace.

While my sister fought her breast cancer, I dialogued with my fear off and on for the next nine years. My conversations with my fear changed as the years went by, and I found more and more insights hiding under my fears. Sometimes this dialogue practice was the only thing that kept me from falling apart completely. Julie and I agreed that we would be brave together. We were fierce about it. We supported each other through it all. We had times when things looked like they might be getting better, and we celebrated. We had times where things turned scary and we had to face our fears again and again—but our fears never went away. Neither did Julie's cancer, but we didn't let our fears define our conversations or our relationship, nor did we ever, ever, ever make decisions or choices based on our fears. We discovered that the antidote to our fear was our love for each other. Instead of spending our time together telling each other scary stories (which would have been easy to do), we practiced loving each other and being brave. We agreed to use our fears to remind us of how much we cared and we left nothing unsaid. And when that awful day arrived and I lost my sister to breast cancer, I knew that my love for her had triumphed over my fear. She knew how much I loved her and how much she would be missed. We had changed our fear into lessons of love. This dialogue practice may seem a bit awkward to you at first, but I found it to be one of the most powerful tools I have for observing emotions and managing fear: my own and my clients'. I also learned that one must never make any decision during moments of fear. Wait for the fear to ease and clear thinking to return before choosing any direction.

Your Choice: *Fear or Love?*

I have heard it said many times that hate is the opposite of love, but I disagree. Fear is the opposite of love. Fear contracts; it tightens and grips. It is cold and frozen. We shiver and shake. We become paralyzed. We feel alone and isolated. In fear's presence, we shrink.

Animals cower and whine—and so do we! Love is the opposite. In love's presence we relax and stretch. We breathe deeply and sometimes sigh. Our muscles loosen, and so do our hearts. We smile. We feel warm; we laugh. It is like the sun coming out on a snowy day—even the ice crystals in the snow sparkle. Love is abundant; it is eternal. And here is the most important thing: Love is the proof that we are spiritual beings. We are expressions of love: giving it or accepting it defines our deepest motivations and purpose for being alive. Love does not die when our bodies die; love grows. I have found myself loving my sister more and more as the years pass without her.

Though you might wish to, you probably won't lose your fear completely. As long as you have this physical body, you will probably experience some form of fear. With practice, however, your fear can stop being your base of operations. Fear doesn't have to paralyze you. You don't have to let it hold you back from achieving your goals, loving your life, and living your dreams. You can investigate it, interview it and find ways to ease its icy grip. If you can switch off your fear-based stories to author new stories based in love, your entire perspective will change. Can you feel yourself relax and expand as you think about moving away from your fear into love? What if the next time you caught yourself feeling afraid of something, and you started up the story-telling projector on your view screen, you pushed the pause button and asked yourself instead: what is the most loving thing I can do in this moment? What is the fear I can address with love? What if you used your own flashlight to shine your love on the fears you have imagined, and the fears that are real? You can use your own loving energy to reassure yourself that your life does not have to be defined by fear, but instead it can be defined by love, hope and acceptance. You can imagine flowers under your bed, instead of the monster!

I found a quartz crystal that really caught my attention, and I noticed how it reflected the light so beautifully. Like any quartz, it was mostly clear with some small facets on its sides. As I turned it, I realized that the source of the reflected light I was admiring was actually a flaw deep inside its core. The crystal contained a fracture, but that was what caught the light. Its brokenness was also its loveliness. We don't have to be perfect to let our light shine and to reflect the light to others around us. The more cracks and fractures and imperfections we have, the more fears we can master, the more loveliness we have to share with others. In our brokenness, we have glimpses through the cracks to the love waiting beyond our story-telling view screens. If we can remember that our truest nature is born from love, returning to love, then perhaps our work here is to quiet the stories on our view screens and see the world without the story-telling. In doing so, we can find our way out into loving the miracle of our own essential truth.

CHAPTER 2

The World is Full of Potato Chips

During my teenage years, our family tradition was to gather Saturday evening to watch the NBC movie on TV. On those nights when we were all at home, and all interested in what was showing, my mother, brother, sister and I would watch it together. We would settle in for the movie and tackle the inevitable issue of snacks. One of us would suggest popcorn (a standard selection), one of us would suggest apples and caramels (my mother's favorite), or my mother might dazzle us by offering us a precious bag of potato chips. Potato chips were an unusual item in our household. They were all the more precious to us because they were rare. We all had differing tastes: Julie preferred the BBQ flavored chips to the regular, plain ones; David liked both, but I actually preferred the plain ones. This was back in the days before the invention of SUPER-size anything, and three teenagers with one bag of chips was a model for scarcity. So, on the evenings when we had potato chips, we had a careful and elaborate system for dividing the bag. If our mother didn't want any, we would distribute the chips between three cereal bowls. My brother often insisted on counting them chip by chip, but Julie and I were more approximate in our measurements. I doled them out in handfuls, while she checked the weight of the bowls when I finished. It seemed like we never had enough. We would all reach the bottom of our individual bowls too soon, and drag our fingers across the surface searching for every bit of salty flavor left there.

One Saturday evening, we were finishing our bowls of potato chips and beginning to argue about who would get the chip "dust" at the bottom of the bag. David had already stood up to retrieve the bag. Julie and I were tensed and ready for battle, when my mother came into the kitchen. She went over to the pantry and quietly pulled out three fresh bags of chips: one of them was the BBQ flavor! We watched her in stunned silence, humbled by the unexpected bounty of chips coming towards us. Mom walked over to the couch and matter-of-factly distributed the bags of chips: "One for Laurel, one for David and one for Julie." Julie got the bag of

BBQ chips, of course, and David and I got the plain ones. We sat there looking at those bags as if they were filled with gold instead of potato chips. I wasn't quite sure what to do with my bag, so I just held it lovingly. David immediately tore open his bag and began happily munching his chips. Julie opened her bag, and re-filled her bowl with one serving, wrote her name on the bag and put it away in the pantry.

We started watching the movie again and I was still holding my bag. Several minutes later a commercial came on again, and we started rustling around in the kitchen. David was thirsty. Julie was taking her now empty bowl to the sink, and I was cradling my still unopened bag, when my mother appeared again. We were absolutely dumbstruck to see that she was carrying three more fresh bags of potato chips! "One for Julie, one for David, and one for Laurel," she said as she handed us a second round of unimaginable wealth. This was too much! I had to know what was going on. Had the Earth tipped on its axis? "Mom?" I asked her. "What's going on?" She turned and smiled at me, saying "the world is full of potato chips, Laurel. We can always get more where these came from!" Julie, David and I sat there absorbing that heady idea in silence. The movie came back on and we were distracted away from any further processing of the wisdom my mother had just dispensed. I opened one of my bags and tested a few chips carefully. I wanted to reassure myself that this was happening; the chips were delicious and real. I wasn't dreaming. We watched the movie together, enjoying our potato-chip wealth. I'm sure we were each assessing our riches in our own private ways. None of us opened the second bag that evening. In fact, after those few chips, I put away my bag. "The world really IS full of potato chips," I thought. "I have enough!" Then, an equally startling thought flashed across my mind: "I wonder what ELSE the world might be full of? I wonder if this feeling of having enough might be all around me."

What is Enough?

What are your stories around scarcity? Where are you feeling scarce in your life? What is your current relationship with wanting and having? Does the following formula apply to you? I want something + I have something = I am happy. If you are telling yourself that you can't be happy until you have something, it becomes very important to know what that something actually is. If you don't know, then spend some time listening to your deep desires and pay attention. The clinical definition for depression is: to want something you don't have. If you don't even know what you want, you have just compounded the possibility of your own sadness and depression. How might your life be different if you stopped letting your feelings of scarcity define your happiness? How might your life be different if you allowed yourself to want, to earn and to enjoy ALL that you dream of having?

When I began working on the idea for this book, the whole notion of having enough was central to my thinking. After years of coaching leaders at various companies around the world, I saw this as an emerging theme of my work. The polarity between scarcity and abundance seemed to be at the core of every individual's ability to grow and transform. My experience had given me a view into leadership, but I was curious to hear from "regular people—" the people on the street. I decided to put together a short survey of questions about "enough." I drove down to my local mall one Saturday morning, and I began interviewing people. I was a woman on a mission to gain a clearer understanding of scarcity afoot in the community. I approached the friendly-looking people and asked the following questions. These are the results of that informal survey:

Question: Do you know the definition of the word "enough"? (Yes or No)

Answer: If yes—what is it? (Verify that their definition agrees with dictionary)

Answer: If no—not applicable, everyone I asked already knew the correct definition.

Question: Do you have enough of everything you want to be happy?

Answer: If yes—not applicable, no one said yes.

Answer: If no—what do you need more of to be happy?

We'll talk about all those answers in a moment, but as you may have guessed already, the #1 answer was money.

Question: How much <insert needed item here> do you need to feel like you have enough?

Answer: Most common answer: 10 million dollars.

Question: Ok—now imagine you have 10 million dollars. Is that enough?
Answer: Oh yes—that's enough. That's plenty! (lots of happy smiles, laughter, instant joy)

Question: Are you happy now?

Answer: Yes—very happy!

Question: Do you want more?

Answer: Oh yes! I'd like more. (Said without hesitation)

Question: So, 10 million dollars was NOT enough?

Answer: Yes—10 million dollars was enough, but I'd still like more.

Question: Would you be happier if you had more than 10 million dollars?

Answer: I am happy with 10 million dollars, but having more would make me even happier.

Question: Is 20 million dollars enough?

Answer: Yes! THAT would be enough!

Question: Ok— now imagine that you have 20 million dollars—do you want more?

Answer: Yes . . .

...And so it went! Every time I doubled the amount of money, the person being interviewed would agree that it was enough, but in the next breath would agree to take more. So, enough wasn't really enough. One gentleman jumped right to infinity on the first question of amount. He said, "I would like to have an endless supply of money for the rest of my life." (He had obviously been doing some thinking about it!)

As I mentioned earlier, the #1 answer to the original question (what do you need more of to be happy in your life) was money. The #2 answer was time, but it wasn't a close second. 58 of the 63 people I spoke to chose money as their necessary item for happiness; four people chose time and only one told me she wished to have more friends. I went home to process these somewhat surprising results. I say somewhat surprising, because I had expected to find more satisfaction in the interviewees once they could imagine having what they wanted. I was surprised to find that most of them (99%) still wanted more—even those who wanted more time said they would happier with double the amount of time they had originally suggested would be enough. Clearly, I had touched a nerve of something universally true, but my own thinking about it was still clouded by notions of wealth and money. I knew that money would not be the key to unlock the mysteries of abundance, so

I kept looking. What is it about money that keeps us so distracted and enthralled? Why was enough—NOT enough?

Scarcity is Learned

Like fear, the feeling of scarcity, that feeling of not having enough, comes to all of us. First, it comes as a chill and then as a tightening and then it triggers fear and panic. Feelings of scarcity don't stop with fear and panic. They grow into clinging and competition. Like the seagulls in *Finding Nemo*, we grab onto our possessions with a throaty cry of "mine!" We cling to our ownership of things as if it were a shield to protect us from emptiness and destruction. You don't have to look too far to find reasons for feeling this way. The world teaches us scarcity, just as it teaches us to fear and to forget our truest nature. Scarcity is all around us, isn't it? The truth is that the recent economic downturn has us fearing for our most basic needs. The collective fear of losing both food and shelter, of living in destitution, has many of us running scared. People are losing their jobs. They are losing their homes. Not since the depression in the 1930's have we experienced this kind of national awareness of scarcity. Even globally we read about countries' financial systems failing: Greece, Germany, Spain, and Iceland just to name a few. We hear news stories about the end of fossil fuels, sky-rocketing gas prices and global warming. We are losing the polar ice caps and animals are going extinct. We don't have enough clean food, clean water, safe homes, jobs, clean air, clean energy, and much more—scarcity surrounds us. It is no wonder, then, that our first answer to the question of wanting something more is to say money. Money is our most highly evolved tool, so it's natural to want to reach for it.

Abundance NOT Money

In order to talk about true abundance, we must acknowledge the elephant in the room: money. As we saw in the previous example, money is often the first stop in any conversation about abundance, so we must dislodge our idea of money in order to see the truth about abundance. While money is a wonderfully flexible tool, it is not the only tool. Is there a way to excavate your feelings of abundance from underneath the weight and distraction of money? Do you believe that you MUST have money in order to experience abundance? One way to find out if you can think beyond money is to allow yourself to embrace that urge. Perhaps by embracing your desire for money, you can temporarily release its grip on your thinking and find what is underneath it? Here is a game I love to play with my clients that may help you embrace the feeling of abundance that lives underneath the weight of money. Ironically, by imagining financial wealth, you can soothe the burn of scarcity and loosen the hold that money has on your deeper, truer abundance. Let's test this idea with the following exercise:

Imagine you have just won the lottery—50 million dollars!! Congratulations! Did I mention it was tax-free? It is! You have 50 million dollars all to yourself. Let the wonderful feeling of total relaxation seep through your body and mind. Release all the fears you held around scarcity. You will never have to worry about money again—ever! You have enough money! No more sleepless nights! The stack of bills on the desk—gone! That mortgage payment staring at you every month— gone! The car on its last leg—gone! Your family is safe. Your children will be cared for, and educated. You will always have a home, and food. You will be able to do things that you thought you might never do. 50 million dollars is all yours. Just relax into knowing that. How are you imagining that money? Pay attention to your body as you sit in your chair imagining the wealth of

50 million dollars. Are you feeling the abundance of it, yet?

Now, what will you do? Have you started imagining yourself spending it, yet? What will 50 million dollars give you? How will it change your life? In your imagination, pay off all your bills. Now you are debt-free. If you want to go on a shopping spree—do it! Let yourself imagine shopping 'til you drop! Imagine yourself all shopped out. Now what do you want to do? Do you feel like a new person because you have 50 million dollars? Does it change your sense of yourself? Make some notes to yourself as you begin to imagine what you would change in your life. The more you relax into the game, the better your insights will be, so really let yourself go! What would you do first? What is the most important change you would make? That single-most important change in your life—what is it? Imagine yourself making that change. Finally, you have what you want most dearly. If all you can imagine is having a Ferrari, ok then imagine having a Ferrari, then imagine yourself driving it to the new you! Let yourself see where it takes you into your life. When you feel like you have thoroughly visualized the wealth of this change, take a few minutes to write down what this change gave you. Who are you, now? How are you spending your days? After you lie on the beach for a month or two, and grow tired of that, what will you do with the rest of your life? Keep digging!

Trust yourself to discover what is under all those stories you have been telling yourself about money and scarcity. Imagining your own personal wealth can help you excavate your own personal abundance, because in getting the feeling of scarcity out of the way and dislodging you requirements for money, you allow yourself to see other possibilities of what ELSE is abundant in you! If you can feel the moment of relaxation in your imagination without actually winning the lottery, then you can feel that same moment of relaxation anytime you wish—whether you have won the lottery or not. You can look at the stack of bills, take a deep breath, relax and re-connect with that abundant feeling you imagined for yourself. What is the power in this? In doing this, you have created space around your fear and your feelings of scarcity into which spirit can flow. Just like you did with your fears in Chapter 1, you are taking your feeling of scarcity and looking at it as a thing, rather than feeling it as an emotion. From your spiritual center, a center of limitless abundance, you hold a wealth of resources and ideas and intuitions about your own life. Your own spiritual center can tell you this every day, if only you have the ears to hear it.

It is a tremendously freeing moment to realize that

you do not require money to live your dreams. You can live your dreams without having vast sums of money. Many clients come to me looking for more happiness, more freedom, and the permission to live their dreams. They are often shocked and delighted to discover that they don't have to find more money to get what they want. By linking the idea of money to your dreams, you allow scarcity to hold you hostage in fear's prison. If fear is the Great Jailer, then money is the Great Distracter. It is an illusion we all share and agree to hold sacred. It is a collective conspiracy, because we share the illusion that more money will give us our dreams, when, in fact, money is only one tool in a vast selection of tools to use to achieve our dreams. Money, and thinking it is the only answer, is the definition of scarcity. When we limit ourselves to only one answer, and we don't have it, we have just defined our lives by scarcity rather than abundance. Do you feel any inner resistance as you read this? This is a difficult idea to hold, and even as I write this I feel the ground trembling! Society would have us all on the hamster wheel of earning more money to keep our economy thriving. It feeds the fear that runs the machine to keep us from seeing our own abundance.

The American Dream

During my nine years at Microsoft, I saw first-hand the power of the American Dream. Men and women from around the world come to work at that amazing and highly competitive company, because they believe that wealth will unlock their dreams. Stock options and signing bonuses call to them. The parking lot on the main campus is filled with evidence of others' dreams realized: Corvette's, BMW's, and Porsche's fill the spaces. An elaborately casual affluence permeates the lunch room. People wander the halls with cutting edge gadgets, eager to show off their hard-won abundance. The Performance Review cycle in which rewards and bonuses are distributed is a highly anticipated and stressful time in the corporate culture. People commonly struggle to articulate their value in their written performance reviews—the value that translates to cash. Feelings of scarcity are thick in the air like smoke, and the back-biting and competition reach new heights with every new review cycle.

Many of the people I mentored during those years also struggled. The subject of money was a frequent topic in my coaching sessions. In fact, money (and the desire for more) was often the reason people at Microsoft would seek out a mentor. Career success was their ticket to greater rewards, promotions and more money, and they believed that having a mentor would show them the secret path to greater success and wealth. They came to me hoping that I could help them improve the value of their performance in the eyes of their managers and teams. It was a kind of "perception management"—they didn't want to increase their work, just the perception that they were valuable. Those who were perceived as valuable received the greater rewards of bonuses, raises and promotions. Having a mentoring, a being able to reference it on a review gave them higher credibility with their managers. Many believed that mentoring was the proof of their commitment to their work and their company. Ironically, in mentoring with me, they often discovered that money was the least of their true desires. Their American Dream was different than the corporate culture's dream of success.

Test Driving Your Dreams

I met one of these mentees early in my mentoring work. A 30-year-old-woman named Beth came to me destined for true success at Microsoft. She had intelligence, education and tenacity. I was sure she was becoming a fine leader. Beth was a bit distracted when she first came to me, however, because she was sure that having a Mercedes Benz would "take her to the next level." The car would tell others that she was serious about success, and she felt certain that having an SLK would make her happy. She had linked the idea of money to her happiness. The equation: I want a Mercedes + (I must acquire a Mercedes) would = her happiness. The car had become a symbol of her success and personal abundance. We had several conversations in which I tried to dislodge her idea of money from her idea of abundance. Finally, when it became clear that those two ideas were inextricably entwined, I suggested that she go ahead and embrace the idea of owning a Mercedes Benz fully. I told her to go down to the Mercedes dealership and test drive the car. I told her to get all dressed up, to really play the part of a wealthy woman looking for this car. I told her to "own" the car completely. At first she was doubtful about the whole idea, but as she prepared to go, she grew more and more enthusiastic. She spent an entire morning dressing. She chose a beautiful dress and shoes to wear. She carefully put on her makeup and fixed her hair. She felt pampered and beautiful as she left for the dealership. She told me about her experience during our next meeting.

When she arrived at the dealership the salesman met Beth at her car. He opened her door for her, and treated her like royalty. Apparently, he was assigned to her for the duration of the contact and he lavished his attention on her. He gave her expensive bottled water, and delicious snacks. Delighted to discover that she worked at Microsoft, he interviewed her to discover her driving habits, her preferences and the pros and cons of which models she might be interested in the most. He encouraged her to test drive three different cars. She told him that she felt a bit guilty for taking so much of his time and she admitted that she wasn't ready to buy, but the salesman reassured her. "It doesn't matter if you're ready to buy today or not. I love talking about these cars! After all," he told her, "you may be ready to buy some other day, and you'll think of us." So Beth let herself relax into the experience, feeling the ownership and wealth first-hand. She let herself bask in the glory of driving those beautiful cars: the fresh, new-car smell, the impeccable interiors, the quiet purr of those engines. By the end of the afternoon, Beth was filled with a fresh appreciation for fine cars, and fine customer service. The salesman thanked her for coming in to the dealership and for giving him the chance to show off his wonderful machines.

As we talked about it, Beth told me that the whole experience helped her realize her dream. She had let herself own those cars during her time at the dealership.

She had let herself feel what it might be like to be that woman driving the SLK 350. She let herself be that woman people looked at and admired: the woman who took her success seriously. "It's funny," she told me. "Now that I have had that experience, I'm not sure I need to actually buy a Mercedes Benz. I mean, they are great cars, but I don't need a car to show people that I'm successful. I know I'm successful. My friends, who really know me, know I'm successful. Why should I buy a car to show strangers that I'm successful?"

Beth had let herself feel the delicious freedom of having something she really wanted. But, she had also realized that having the car didn't change who she was. She had found something inside herself which was far more valuable than a car. She realized that she didn't have to wait for a Mercedes Benz to be happy. She decided that she could be happy now. She wanted a newer car, and could already afford one even if it wasn't a Benz. She set about looking for something sportier, and newer with an impeccable interior. She found a beautiful previously owned car, but more than that, she freed herself from the mindset that money is the source of her happiness. Now, don't get me wrong—this is not to say that buying an expensive car is unnecessary. Any decision you make about your purchases is entirely up to you. The point here is to see that having large sums of money is not necessary to feeling happy. With a little creativity, you can give yourself many of the things that will make you happy. You can find your own version of the bag of potato chips to lavish upon yourself without having vast wealth.

Now that Beth has stopped feeling imprisoned by her own ideas about money she has started to look for ways to creatively integrate that feeling of abundance into her life. She gives herself spa days at home, or takes her husband out for a martini with her spike heels on, or sits in an obliging field on a lawn chair she brought from home to enjoy a big sky feeling. Her career continues to be successful and rewarding in ways that she could not have anticipated. At work, she continues to enjoy success, rewards and promotions. Once she disconnected her idea of happiness from her idea of the symbol of her success, she discovered that she was already enjoying tremendous success and approval from her management team. She had blinded herself to the truth of her own happiness with stories of her own scarcity. Once she silenced those stories, she could see her success much more clearly.

Conscious Living and
True Abundance

Would it surprise you to discover that you are holding yourself hostage in your own private prison of scarcity? You blind yourself to all the other available opportunities by limiting your perspective to thinking that money is the only escape. You are telling yourself that story and still you are surprised when it becomes real. While it is true that money is sometimes helpful, it is also true that sometimes it only gets in the way. In fact, true abundance has very little to do with money. The world is full of whatever you need, if you can allow yourself to see it, and give yourself permission to reach for it. I know this is a ground-shaking idea, but relax, breathe and remember that you are the Awareness. Money flows in and out of your life, but abundance is always with you. Finding abundance may be as simple as asking for help from your friends. It may be as simple as taking a deep breath. We are as wealthy as the relationships we foster. We hold the entire Universe in our Awareness inside the view screen. If you can turn off the frightening stories of scarcity, you will see all the world waiting beyond the story.

In my talks, I often use the example of driving a car to explain the difference between conscious living and being on auto-pilot. Conscious living is keeping your Awareness—your Truest Self in the driver's seat. It means making choices in alignment with a deeper sense of spirit. Your Truest Self, the part of you that is fully awake to the experiences around you gives you access to a great deal of information: physical, emotional, mental and spiritual. You see the road ahead with all that information pouring in, and you choose, consciously, which turns and lanes to take. When your Story-Teller is in the driver's seat, though, you cannot see the road ahead. Your Story-Teller keeps your stories running with the pre-programmed instructions from your view screens. It distracts you and clouds your view of the world, and limits the information you could be receiving. With the Story-Teller is in the driver's seat, you are not really engaged in actively living your own life. You are living the stories dictated by your view screen. It is important to keep your True Self in the driver's seat, and your story-telling quiet, if you want to access the abundance of information available to you when consciously engaging the world. One way to check where your attention is focused is to ask: Am I happy, engaged and joyful during the day? Or, Do I feel lonely and isolated, fearing that doom is waiting around the next corner? The endless story-telling has a way of keeping you blind to all the opportunities for abundance in your life. The endless barrage of stories from your private viewing screens keeps you locked in old, self-limiting behaviors and patterns of scarcity.

A Wealth of Pot Stickers

I remember another lesson I had in abundance when my son, Tyler, and I had just moved to Seattle to work for Microsoft. Leaving a 10-year career as a teacher, I consciously chose to take a pay cut of 9K dollars a year. I believed that my future prospects were better in corporate America than they had been in academia, so I bit the bullet, re-engineered my budget, and moved our little family to Redmond, WA. Those first few months were difficult financially, and although I was watching my bottom line very carefully we had times when we simply ran out of money—that is, we only had $5.00 left in the checking account. One Friday night, I came home tired and fearing the inevitable look through the cupboards for food I knew wasn't there. I found a bag of rice, some carrots and a carton of milk in the refrigerator and a box of cereal. Tyler, a healthy 8-year-old boy, was hungry and I was starting to feel that icy grip of scarcity. I looked at the rice, and had a semi-brilliant idea: we would buy a quart of hot and sour soup from our local favorite Chinese take-out place, and add the rice to it for a Chinese feast.

"Tyler! Let's go on a treasure hunt," I told him. "Let's search the house for all the coins we can find. I bet there's some in the couch cushions."

"I know there's some out in the car, Mom! You always keep quarters in the tray for the parking meters!" said Tyler, excited to play this new game.

Sure enough, we managed to scrape together over six dollars in change from around the house. We drove down to the Chinese restaurant to place our order, and were met by our favorite hostess. She had made friends with Tyler when we first came to Redmond, and we had been going to her restaurant regularly for the past few months. Tyler proudly announced to her that we had $6.00 to spend on our dinner that night and she looked at me with such tender smile that it almost made me cry. She patted Tyler's hand and asked us to sit down to wait for a moment. She made no mention of the $6.00; she came back a few minutes later with a large cardboard box filled with little take-out cartons of food! Tyler jumped up and said "Oh no, we only have $6.00!" She just smiled and told us she was having a dinner special, and this was the $6.00 meal for two. It was far more food than we could ever eat in one meal. We thanked her, and thanked her and thanked her again, and took our feast home to enjoy that night and for three more nights to come. When we opened the cartons at home, we realized that she had given us all the favorites we would have ordered if we had more money. Tyler, delighted with the sudden wealth of pot stickers and noodles, and well-versed in the family lore of the potato chip story, laughed out loud when he saw the feast of favorites before us. "Look Mom," he said. "Now the world is full of Chinese food!" –and so it was! We had not gone to the Chinese restaurant looking for such generosity. We went because we refused to let the $6.00 in change define our personal wealth. We refused to feel scarce even in the face of our empty pockets. We were met with kindness, and generosity, confirming for us that the world was an abundant place, after all. Had we created that abundance? –or was it already there for us to discover? We might never have known if we had let our story of scarcity keep us locked in our fear.

Tool: Visualize Your True Abundance

Here is a simple exercise to help you loosen the grip of scarcity from your thinking. It can help you feel abundant in a different way.

Find a quiet, comfortable place to sit. Close your

eyes and begin taking slow, deep breaths. You may even want to count at first to make sure you are breathing slowly. Breathe in 1, 2, 3, 4 through your nose and breathe out 1, 2, 3, 4 through your mouth. As you establish this slower rhythm, focus your attention on your Awareness in the chair. Let your view screens grow quiet and begin to picture, instead, that you are breathing in abundance. Imagine that your breath is your life and you are breathing it in deeply. Picture your body being fed by this oxygen. Now exhale through your mouth and picture all the fear and scarcity leaving you. You are filling up with abundance and emptying yourself of fear. Picture all your worries about scarcity flying right out of your mouth and disappearing like steam into the air. Breathe out the fear of the mortgage. Breathe in relaxation. Breathe out the fear of losing your job. Breathe in trust and confidence in your ability. Breathe out to release the scarcity; Breathe in to fill yourself with abundance. Do this for as long as it takes to feel completely full of abundance. Breathe in until you feel as if you will burst with abundance if you take another sip of this wonderful elixir! Do you have enough air? Of course, you do! Every breath you take is abundance, and there is plenty more where that came from.

Now picture yourself breathing in light. At first this light is misty, but instead of it being comprised of water molecules, it is filled with light molecules instead. As you breathe in you become weightless. You can see yourself actually lifting out of your chair. As you breathe, and as you lift higher and higher, the light mist becomes denser and brighter. Soon it becomes so dense that you cannot even see your arms, legs and feet. You dissolve into the cloud of light; you are the light—breathe it in and shine. You are totally at peace, relaxed and abundant. You want nothing—there is nothing to want in this radiant peace. This is what you have yearned for and finally found. This is the voice that whispers in the back of your mind. This is the connection that is behind all the other things you want. Let this quiet, peaceful cloud of light in which you have everything you need fill you as if you were a thirsty sponge. Feel it saturate you. Let every cell of your body soak up the light and radiance of this cloud. Breathe in; breathe out. This is abundance. Do you have enough air? Of course you do!

And if, in this moment, you can clear your screen of all your stories of scarcity, fear and yearning, your view screen will surely open and you will see the world, unobstructed. You will see what binds us all together. You will see the love that permeates us all.

This is the essential, abundant connection to your spiritual self; re-connecting to this limitless source of love and peace can set many other things in motion in your life. Opportunities arise from this connection that you did not see before. Indeed, your perspective changes because you are conscious of this connection now. You may find yourself no longer wanting some of those things that you thought were so important and necessary to your happiness before. You may see new ways to find satisfaction with yourself and your relationships. New people may arrive or old friends may re-visit you who can help you and teach you new things about yourself. Why do you doubt the connection? You are a spirit; you are here to have this physical experience and to learn from it. You are here to bring all of that loving energy into your body and into your life. Your story about scarcity is only a distraction. So much information is available to you when you push aside the old stories and see the world in all its radiant and abundant possibility. What might your life be like if you lived connected to this deeper sense of abundance every day? What might you be able to create for yourself that reflects this deeper understanding?

Your Choice: Putting Abundance in its Place

This is the challenge which abundance offers you:

you can stay in the stasis of the old story, running around the same old racetrack. It's comfortable and familiar, I suppose, and you're not a bad person to think of staying there. You know the terrain. You know all the stories and players, and you never expect more of yourself than to tell those stories over and over again. But, what about that yearning you feel? What about that quiet voice that asks: isn't there something more? It is your Awareness, your Truest Self surrounded by all those view screens. You stay there watching all those stories, and the problem with staying in that old, story-telling place inside your curtain is that you are not consciously connected to abundance. You are not consciously connected to the pure joy of your own essential truth. You are not consciously connected to the creative energy of the spirit which defines you. The truth is that you are the author of your own life and not just a character in the stories you project on screen. You can re-write, re-imagine and re-create yourself in connection with your True Self: your radiant self to live the abundant life of your dreams! You put abundance in its place every time you remember that it is always and already around you. By placing it center stage in your life, you change your life in the process.

This is the true abundance you yearn for day-to-day. It is the truth under your desires: the things you think you need to be happy. Yearning pulls you to your True Self, the Awareness in the chair: your divine and essential nature. When you embrace the yearning and re-connect with the total abundance of your spiritual nature, you see the world in an entirely new way. The world becomes full of whatever you need: potato chips, Chinese food, friendships and most of all—love. When you find your connection to the abundance of your spiritual self, your view screens will go mute; your curtain will become more transparent and you will push aside those old stories to see your own truest things: to see the miracle of the life you are truly here to live.

"When you're tired and you can't sleep, just count your blessings instead of sheep—and you'll fall asleep counting your blessings!"—Irving Berlin

CHAPTER 3

Be True! Be True! Be True!

I don't know how many high school students I have taught during my years as a teacher. In twelve years of teaching, with 3-5 classes of 11th graders, with 35-40 students in each class, I suppose it is over 2000 students. Each year, the standard curriculum required me to teach *The Scarlet Letter*, by Nathaniel Hawthorne. Each year, I tried to bring to life this amazing story about the struggle of a man who wanted to live an authentic life, defined by openness, honesty and love, yet who failed so miserably. I loved the complex idea that this "Godly man" was actually one of the biggest "sinners" in the story— living completely out of alignment with the philosophies and religious beliefs he so devoutly espoused, instead of living in harmony with the deeper truth of love. I read this novel as a rich, albeit tragic, story of the human dilemma we all face in one way or another, trying to reconcile the public roles we play against the private truth we yearn for.

My students were frequently surprised by the passion I felt when teaching this novel. They could see how much I loved it. We had spirited debates about its modern-day relevance and the myriad examples around us of other "lost souls:" men and women who were searching for the reconciliation of their own public and private selves: reconciling the roles they play with some truer part of themselves. My students did not understand how I could overlook Hawthorne's florid, 19th Century vocabulary and the overwhelming dogma of the Puritan church in favor of seeing simple truth in it. Little did they know that I loved this novel, because I *lived* the lesson of this novel during the course of my first marriage. Not because I was like any one of the characters in the story, but because I, too, struggled with the folly of choosing a highly polished, story-driven, public life over something more authentic. I mistakenly believed that being a wife would fulfill my own personal dreams of love. I allowed my story-telling to take me down a road defined by a collective agenda; one which dictated marriage, family, and motherhood. I chose in favor of a life defined by those roles, those stories, instead of a life defined by love. In my fear of losing my chance for love, I reached for something that was completely false, and in doing so, stepped away from a deeper life of authenticity. I did not know that reconciling the gap between my own public and private self would become so important. Ironically, I had ignored Hawthorne's warning at the end of the *The Scarlet Letter*. He tells us: "Be true! Be true! Be true! Show freely to the world, if not your worst, yet some trait whereby the worst may be inferred!"

As Hester Prynne told the magistrates of Boston, "I cannot speak the sins of another; I can only speak my own." Taking away the drama of her Puritan lens, I still appreciate the wisdom in taking responsibility for my own mistakes. Blaming my ex-husband would be like pointing into a mirror and finding my own shortcomings. Wouldn't it be wonderfully easy if I could just blame him and walk away? In doing so, however, I would lose a rich opportunity to take back my own personal power and learning. If I am not a part of the problem, I cannot be a part of the solution, and so I look more closely at the story of our failed marriage for the truth underneath it. As embarrassing as it might be to do this in public, I consider this a part of "being true:" true to myself, true to my reader and true to the world.

The Life I Learned With

As the new Single's Pastor at my church in San Diego, my ex-husband was a pleasure to know. He seemed like one of us—-so authentic and friendly. As Pastor, Tony was charming, funny, and laughed easily at himself. He had a wife and two sons, but still managed to keep his congregation at the center of his attention. He seemed devoted to our spiritual growth, and dedicated to a higher calling. Since I was an English teacher, it was natural for me to help write the Singles' monthly newsletter. As Singles Pastor, Tony had a regular column in the newsletter, so I worked with him, editing his writing, laughing about his mistakes and word choice and enjoying the whole process of producing the newsletter. Tony wanted me to join the Single's Leadership Council, so I began spending more of my spare time at church and with him. Writing newsletters led to attending conferences and spending more time together. By the end of the summer it was clear to me that Tony had stronger feelings for me than friendship.

I remember the day Tony sat on my couch and told me about his feelings for me. I felt sick to my stomach and shaky at the time—a feeling I later learned was a signal from my True Self to stop and consider. At the time, I thought it was just the guilt I felt for having a

LAUREL A. ROSS, PhD

82

conversation like this with a married man. I asked him about his wife and sons and he told me that a love like ours answered to a higher authority. Looking back, I wonder how I could have been so gullible and so needy, but I was a different person, then. At 27, I had already begun to feel the pressure of being unmarried. I could hear my own clock ticking and was flattered by his attention and the grandiosity of his vision for our life together. The public man, the Singles' Pastor of my church, was asking me to marry him! I could scarcely wrap my mind around it, and I let myself be drawn into it because I wanted a love of my own. I wanted to be a wife and to have a husband. I wanted to believe that we could come together with impunity, undeterred by his wife and family. If my Self today could go back and talk to the young woman I was, I would tell her to run! I would tell her that taking her happiness at the cost of causing others pain was never a good idea. I would warn her about the price she would have to pay for choosing to follow a life defined by her roles, rather than a life defined by love. I would ask her to not to make her choice based on fear: the fear of being alone.

Months passed, Tony began to implement, what he called, his Master Plan. He left his wife, his family, the church and found a new job. He changed everything about his life in order to have me with him. I remember feeling tremendous guilt about all those changes through the early months of our courtship. Tony was starting to show signs of irritability and anger during our private time together. I dismissed it all to stress. I believed that when we married, we would settle into a quieter and more peaceful routine, and begin to live the life he had outlined for me on that first afternoon. I was working as a full-time teacher and trying to integrate him into my life at the high school. The other faculty seemed impressed with him, and the fact that I was now engaged gave me a feeling of pride about fitting into a community. I was a successful, upwardly-mobile, young woman about to join the "club" of married women and eventually, mothers. I felt all the excitement of stepping up to this new level of my own social development. My sense of authenticity was quite buried under the new role I was taking on. I had some vague whisperings from my higher self about the possibility that we might be moving too fast, but Tony was always there to calm those fears and to apologize for his irritability.

The first time Tony hit me, I knew I was more shocked than physically hurt. After a dinner party with friends, I was trying to check on the messages from my phone machine. In his jealousy and rage, he shoved me to the floor, knocking over the phone table and breaking my answering machine. The second time Tony hit me was after we were married and I discovered that he had lied to me about the authenticity of our marriage certificate. In his anger, he grabbed me so hard that I had bruises on my arm in the shape of his fingers. His irritability had escalated from yelling to shoving to grabbing and finally to "thumping." He would thump on my breast bone with his index finger to punctuate his points as he yelled at me, leaving bruised tattoo-marks.

I felt like I was living in a kind of Twilight Zone: in public we were the happy, loving couple so devoted to each other, living our dreams. At home, we were living a nightmare. I wanted to be a good wife, so I started seeing a therapist at our new church, hoping to find some guidance to navigate these treacherous waters. The life I had imagined for myself was very different from the one I was living, and though I didn't have the words to describe that, I see now that I was starting to see my own gap between the role I had chosen and the life I had dreamed of. I didn't tell my therapist about the cycles of abuse, but I was starting to wake up to the fact that I had abandoned myself in the course of our relationship. In therapy, I realized that I had lost so much of the girl I was before I married Tony that I scarcely recognized my Self anymore.

And Baby Makes Three

In my role confusion, I mistakenly reasoned that one role's failure could be redeemed by taking on another role, and so I decided to have a baby. I actually thought it might help to calm down Tony. It seems ludicrous to me, now, to write something so blatantly foolish, but I truly believed in the power of the roles I was trying to play. My stories told me that the roles could work, if I could only learn how to master them more effectively. Hundreds of men and women were happily married, weren't they? Surely, I could be happy, too. I was trying to live a normal life, trying to be obedient to my husband and trying to be a decent woman. I reasoned that all of the abuse stemmed from my own flaws. Surely, I MUST be the cause of the abuse—how else could I make it stop? I believed that if I was careful enough, I could keep Tony calm; at the time, having a baby seemed like a reasonable solution to me. Perhaps, I told myself, reminding Tony of his role as a father would help bring a measure of peace back into our lives.

The violence stopped while I was pregnant, but returned within a few months after Tyler was born. I do not need to catalog all the offenses—that is not the point. I was allowing the abuse because I believed that I was the cause of it. I was like a gambler who had placed a big bet, and I was determined to see it pay off. I believed I could help Tony. I had grown accustomed to being successful in many other ways, so it was natural for me to believe that I could "tough it out" and "bring him around." So, I hid the bruises at work. I stopped seeing my family as often. I didn't talk to my sister about any of it. Like all the struggling characters in *The Scarlet Letter*, I kept my secret——I hid my shame. I was "in" my story completely. Who knows how long I might have stayed in this story: this nightmare of a marriage? Who knows how far I would have let it go? I sometimes asked myself why I thought I was so undeserving of love. Why did I allow so much abuse? Clearly, I was more afraid of leaving Tony and being alone than I was of staying . . . until that fateful day when Tony's rage turned towards Tyler!

Time to Wake Up!

Tyler was just past his first birthday, and still a bit wobbly on his legs. We had celebrated "Mister One" a few weeks earlier with Tyler's first steps but he was still using various objects to pull himself upright before he would walk. He used everything: couches, footstools, my leg, and Tony's. One morning, as Tony was preparing to leave the house, Tyler crawled over to him and used his dress pant leg as his handle to stand up. Tyler's hands were spitty and wet from his baby chores, and they left a wet mark on Tony's pant leg. In his disgust and irritation, Tony thrashed out his leg in a kicking motion and sent Tyler literally flying through the air. It was as if time stopped as I watched in total horror as my little boy took flight across the living room floor. All the questions, musings and intuitions I had flashed across my mind in perfect clarity. I knew in that moment that this was NOT my life. This was NOT the life I intended to live, nor wanted to live. My life defined by the story of the "good wife" was over. Tyler landed on a pile of pillows I kept there to protect him from the brick edge of the fireplace hearth. He landed in a surprised "thump," not hurt, not crying—just stunned. Tony stormed upstairs to change his pants and left for work. Some kind of a switch went "click" in my head. Within an hour, I had packed two bags, called in sick at work, and gassed up the car on the road to my grandparents' house. I felt quietly calm in my resolve. I felt like I was awake for the first time in years, and I saw everything that I had forgotten about myself while I was playing the role of "wife." Life had given me the rare and sudden gift of an empty view screen. My stories were silent. In that silence, I saw how I had forgotten to love myself, and

LAUREL A. ROSS, PhD

listen to myself and the truth had finally set me free. I spent the weekend with my grandparents, my mother and my sister brainstorming how to leave Tony without getting hurt.

From There to Here

The logistics of ending my marriage were simple enough. The hardest thing, we all agreed, was going to be the moment I told him. My mother gave me some advice that has proved so helpful in other situations through the years. She said, "You only have to be strong for a few minutes, Laurel—and you only have to tell him once." I knew that I could be strong for a few minutes for Tyler's sake and for the sake of my own truth. I decided to tell Tony I was leaving him during our scheduled counseling session at the church. I had fore-warned our therapist about what I was doing and he suggested that I tell Tony and then leave immediately, as a safeguard against potential violence. I had Tyler with me at the appointment. The receptionist kept an eye on him for the 5 strong minutes it took me to make my announcement. Tony was stone-faced. I left quickly before he could start yelling. I moved out of the house the following weekend with the help of my students and a small army of trucks. I had rented a condo closer to my school, and Tyler's daycare was just up the street. I had escaped. I closed the door on my first apartment with Tyler and felt Hester's freedom as she took off her *A* in the forest. Like Hester, "I did not know the weight until I felt the freedom."

Within a year, Tony had signed away all of his parental rights to Tyler. He didn't want to pay child support, and I was more than happy to free him of any obligations which required Tyler to spend time with him. I was happy to be a single parent at 32, raising my son alone. After a few strained visits with Tony, from which Tyler came home filthy and tired, I was happy to keep my son with me—to keep Tyler safe. I had exchanged my role as Tony's wife—the public self I had been building—for a truer life of loving my son and re-discovering the woman I am today.

Though one could argue that motherhood is another set of stories (and it is), it is also a truer expression of my loving self, one which I consciously live. That role, that collection of stories, helped me to see that my life could only be defined by love, and not by the role I played. In loving my son, I found a new way to love myself and forgive myself for the pain I had caused others, caused myself and caused Tyler. Love pointed me back to a truer sense of myself. I closed the gap between the public-image of "mother" by aligning my intention to love my son with loving actions in my behavior. In fact, I closed the gap of needing to be anything other than my Self. I used my energy to "be true" to myself rather than to a pre-programmed role and discovered who that Self actually was. I found new strength and new goals for myself. I earned my Master's degree, continued teaching gifted students and began raising Tyler with more joy and more freedom than I had felt before. I realized that I had willingly stayed in that marriage because I believed I could do no better. What I would not do for my own sake, I willingly did for Tyler's. I freed myself from a phony life, defined by my stories, in favor of a richer life defined by love, and in doing so I found tools for returning to my own Awareness—my True Self.

Authenticity: Public and Private

What kind of a gap between public and private self do you experience in your daily life? Do you find yourself thinking one thing and doing another? Do you make choices in favor of what others might think of you? Do you let your story-telling run you? Do you find yourself playing a role in your story rather than being yourself?

How might your life be different if you allowed yourself to live from a truer place within? What would it take to bring you back into alignment with some truer sense of yourself?

The gateway to authenticity lives in the gap between your public and your private self. A gap is a space created by a misalignment between what your Awareness knows and what you are actually living. The gap is created when you allow your public self, the story you show to the world, to become something other than the Awareness inside your viewing screen. When you lose the alignment between your Awareness and your actions, you lose your essential connection to your truth. Authenticity, then, grows out of the re-alignment of your truth with your actions. Carpenters have a term they call "truing up" when they bring a piece of wood, or a line, or a level back into alignment with the design of their building. Authenticity is a kind of personal "truing up" that you undertake when you align your actions and behaviors with your True Self. Put simply: to live authentically in the world, you must behave in alignment with your own truth.

Without taking yourself on a guilt trip, do you know already where you are out of alignment in your own life? I cannot tell you where you may need to "true up" in order to feel the joy of living an authentic life. I cannot tell you whether you are hurting yourself or others by living out of alignment with your own True Self. In fact, I rarely have to tell my clients what their essential truths are; they come to me already knowing. They come to me because the gap between the roles they play, the stories they tell and their private dreams of how life might be becomes too wide to navigate on their own. Our work together often focuses on finding the gateway within the gap and walking through it to their own authentic presence.

Internal, External, Eternal

It is no accident that Hawthorne tells us to Be True three times. By simple repetition he points to an important structure for our own restoration of personal truth. First, we must be true to ourselves: true to our own values and Awareness. Then, we must be true to others: telling our truth and living our truth. Finally, we must be true to the BIG truth: the truth that we are all spiritual beings having this human experience. We are coming from love, manifesting love and returning to love. In the face of this simple three-step admonition, our work becomes clear. We must "true-up:" align ourselves internally, externally, and eternally. But how do we do this?

In a world which elevates the glitz, celebrates the glamour and rewards the fake, how do we find our own measure of authenticity?

The first of Hawthorne's advice: Be True! begins within you. Your Awareness can point the way to begin this internal re-alignment by identifying a value which you hold dear. For the purposes of practicing this re-alignment, choose one value you hold which is currently out of alignment with your daily behavior. If you cannot think of a value, remember to look in the gap between your story and the deeper wishes for your life. Perhaps you value spending time with your family, but you find yourself staying at the office until 7:00 p.m. every evening. Perhaps you value being healthy and fit, but you find yourself eating sugary foods without exercising. Perhaps you value having an education, but find yourself procrastinating about applying to colleges for your degree. Take a look at the following example from one of my client's values identification work. Dave came to see me, troubled by the feeling that he was missing out on his children's childhood, and thinking that he was spending too much time at work. He valued being successful and receiving rewards and bonuses, but he also valued being a loving father and husband. For Dave, "living his dream" was having a successful career, a happy, healthy family, and a loving relationship with his wife. This simple exercise allowed him to see the behaviors he could change in order to live in closer alignment with his values.

Tool: Identify Authentic Values

Whatever the value you hold, write it down at the top of a piece of paper.

This is the value I (Dave) hold: **I value spending time with my family.**

Now write several behaviors that demonstrate this value. In other words, what does this value look like in concrete examples in your life? Remember this is personal, so you get to decide for yourself what this looks like for you.

Dave's Example:

I have dinner with my spouse and children 5 out of 7 nights a week.

I tuck my children into bed 5 out of 7 nights a week.

I sit alone with my spouse talking about our lives at least 30 minutes every day.

I spend at least one day each weekend doing something with my family that we all enjoy: going to the park, seeing a movie, having dinner out, or taking a hike.

I take trips with my family as my vacation time allows away from our house to show my children the natural world: camping, climbing, fishing.[1]

As a part of "truing up" with himself, Dave took each of the values he identified for himself one at a time, and implemented changes over the course of a six-week period. Because he also valued his success at work, Dave decided to talk to his manager about the changes he planned to implement that directly affected his work. He told his boss that he planned to leave the office every day by 6:00 pm, and he asked for his boss's feedback if any of his work seemed to be slipping. He made it clear that he still valued being a profitable employee, but also wanted to live in greater alignment with his own integrity about being a family man. How could his boss deny him this? It turned out that Dave's boss was actually inspired by Dave's commitment to his family and started doing the same thing himself. Soon, other employees in Dave's office were leaving at 6:00, too and heading out to live their lives. He told me how much the morale of the whole office changed as his co-workers began to take time for their own interests after work. It surprised him, at first, the power of his "little idea," but he also recognized that he hadn't been the only one feeling out of alignment.

Interestingly, the company didn't suffer. In fact, the

office (this branch of an insurance company) started showing greater profits and productivity. They won an award and earned greater bonuses for everyone in the office. This was an unintended outcome, of course, but it illustrates the power of one person's efforts to restore an authentic life for himself. He inspired an entire office to do the same. Dave's desire to be a better husband and father influenced an entire branch office to live in greater alignment with their values, too.

The Joy of Your Convictions

Once you begin to explore your own first step towards authenticity you can find myriad opportunities to "true up." Rather than allow yourself to feel phony, you can use the feeling of phoniness to push you back into alignment with your deeper sense of truth. This doesn't have to be a grim process. In many ways, it is a joyful one and taking a humorous approach to it can actually help to relieve you of whatever discomfort you might feel in re-calibrating your relationships and truing them up. No doubt, you will find places in your relationships where you have been a part of situations and conversations that were not in alignment with your True Self.

I frequently hear dissatisfaction in people around allowing themselves to be caught up in gossiping and generally snarky commentary among friends. I once suggested to an audience of young women that they simply tell the truth in those situations. One young woman from the audience asked me: "how do you manage to keep any friends, if you always tell the truth?" It is a funny question, but one that illustrates the kind of backward thinking that can creep in when you avoid closing your own gaps! It is a great example of the old story-telling mechanism that revs up and tries to dictate your behaviors. The story begins with a wave of fear and self-doubt: "what will people think if I don't go along with the group? How can I get out of this uncomfortable situation?" If you remember to Be True to yourself, the answer soon becomes clear. You stop doing things which are not in alignment with your values. That's it—you just stop! Without negotiation, without analysis, without wrapping yourself around the axle, when you find yourself in a situation where you are not being true to yourself—leave. This is the answer to the first "Be True!"

Into the World

We might also answer this young woman's question by posing the reverse question: "how do you manage to keep any friends **without** telling the truth?" How does anyone build a true relationship with another human being without being true? How does gossiping with friends reflect my highest truth? It doesn't! So, I don't do it! That is my value. This is a response to the second Be True: be true to others. That is a value I hold dear. I value loving people as much as I value helping to encourage and inspire them. I can honor all these values at once in any moment by simply asking: what is the most loving thing I can do in this moment? I have not yet heard the answer: "Laurel, you can love them by gossiping about them!" That would be surprising, indeed! Gossiping about my friends is rarely in alignment with my highest truth—or theirs! This is not to say that I always feel loving and accepting of my friends and their choices. I have opinions just like everyone else, but I do not believe it is necessary to express every thought and emotion.

I love the advice my grandmother gave me once when I was struggling with the question of how much I should say: she told me, "Laurel, just ask yourself: is it kind? Is it true? Is it necessary? If it can't pass the test on all three points—don't say it!" My grandmother was actually quoting something she had heard from her affiliation with the Rotary Club, and from Sri Sai Baba— an admonition I have since learned is widely used. It is a litmus test I have used again and again to catch myself. I have found that I sometimes pass two of the three: something that is true and necessary, but may not feel kind. In this case, I trust to my loving intention and say it as kindly as possible. Sometimes, I find that I have something kind and true to say, but it is not necessary to say in that moment, so I wait to say it. Each of us must decide our own criteria for when to speak and what to say, but being mindful of those moments can help to "true-up" our relationships. Passing all three provides an excellent filter and a pointer to the third Be True! Is it necessary? For the sake of *what* am I going to say this?

The BIG Truth

The third repetition of Be True takes us to the BIG truth! Be true to the BIG truth that you are a radiant, spiritual being in the world with other spiritual beings. Whether or not they know it, they, too, are here for the human experience. As long as you remember that BIG truth, you will invite them to remember it by your mere presence. Your connection to spirit and to love will implicitly ask others to join you there. Lest you feel afraid of losing your friends and being alone, let me reassure you that I have found no greater attraction than the attraction of a loving spirit. Because we are all spiritual beings, we innately know the truth of our essential self defined by love. What is the point of phoniness if you can admit to yourself that you are love? This is the connection to the BIG truth of who you truly are: you are the loving Awareness inside your stories. No matter how slick and highly polished those stories you are watching on your view screen might be, they are still only a story: a shadow of your loving essence. They do not show the BIG truth. This may seem like a radical notion: radical, because it is different from the usual or traditional idea of loving. The Awareness, your True Self, loves in spite of the darkness and fear of the stories on the view screen. Your True Self loves radically for the purpose of changing the world: returning the world to its truest state and all the rest of the story-telling, role-playing and phoniness just goes away.

The Road Not Taken

I could have let my old stories and my old mistakes define me and keep me from becoming my True Self. I could have stayed in my first marriage, defined by my role in my story of "wife." The truth is that I had no idea, at that point in my life, what a loving marriage even looked like. I did not know how to be true. I had not yet discovered my own sense of myself and being 27 didn't mean anything. Age has little to do with self-awareness. Looking back, I feel so blessed to have had the experience that taught me where to look for my own authenticity. I feel grateful for the love and support I had from my family to learn and grow into the woman I have become today. Tony, like all of us, is living his own life. I cannot say whether or not he has found his own authenticity, but I wish him well. I cannot wish that I had never met him because I would not have learned without that lesson; I would not have Tyler and I would have needed different lessons to discover my true loving potential. By daring to step out of the role I played, I made room for something more authentic to grow.

The life I live now is far different from the life I learned with. By leaving that old, role-driven story-telling, I made room for something truer to grow. Years later, when Tyler was a teenager, I met my husband, Dan. By then, I knew **my** True Self, so I was able to see **his** True Self. We recognized the BIG love in each other, and becoming husband and wife became a natural expression of that love. We do not define our relationship by the roles we play. We define our lives together with the abundance of love we experience and share. This is the life I had imagined for myself so long ago. This was the truth that was whispering to me in the background as I blindly lived in my story. This love is the love that we all might have for each other, if we can only release those old stories that keep us playing the role, characters in our own story instead of the authors of it.

Your Choice: Love the Gap!

In my coaching I frequently tell my clients to watch for the gaps between the life they want and the life they are living. Whenever I have the pleasure of traveling to London, I love to read the signs on the London Underground which read "Mind the Gap!" I laugh because these signs are such an excellent reminder that the best way to find the authenticity that comes out of re-aligning your True Self with your actions is to "mind the gap." I also like to take this one step further; I like to *love* the gap! You can love the space between where are you are and where you want to be. Your authenticity lives in that gap—so when you notice it (mind it) you can also love it. You can "true up" your intentions first. Do the work to identify what you truly value and then bring it into the world. You will find great joy in the process and true friends who will support you. When you choose to love in this new and radical way, you step into the greatness of the Divine and change your world. Authenticity is not a destination; it is a practice. As we peel back the layers of truth within ourselves, align our truth with our actions and bring more truth into our relationships we will see many other opportunities for change. This moment is only one moment in the practice. In this moment, you can choose to Be true! Be true! Be true!

CHAPTER 4

I Love You Forever!

It was Cinco de Mayo, 2001, and the phone rang. My sister was calling to tell me that our mother was in the emergency room in San Diego with stomach pain, and they were prepping her for exploratory surgery. I was in Seattle; I called the airlines and booked a flight for the following morning. Julie picked me up at the airport and we drove straight to the hospital to meet our younger brother, Tory. Mom was out of surgery; she was groggy, but still able to smile when she saw me. The doctor was waiting for us in the hall. He told us that the exploratory surgery revealed that our mother had extensive abdominal cancer which had infiltrated her liver, stomach, and intestines. He asked us if she had any history of cancer, and we told him that she had breast cancer five years ago, but we thought she had beaten it. He shook his head and told us that the breast cancer had metastasized throughout her abdomen. He started to talk to us about aggressive treatments, radiation and chemotherapy, but cautioned us against having much hope. "We don't usually see the results we'd like to see," he said. He stood with us for a few more moments discussing oncology and suggesting that we talk to our mother about her options, and then he walked away, leaving us in a stunned silence.

I don't remember which one of us spoke first, but when we did we all blurted out comments about how sudden this was and how we had no idea she was even sick. "Does this mean that Mom is going to die?" I asked suddenly. "Is that what he was telling us?" We had more silence, and more shock. I looked over at Julie and Tory, as David, my older brother, came down the hall towards us. Tory took a few minutes to recap what the doctor had told us and it sounded even weirder hearing it the second time. Then he suggested that we go talk to our Mom. The four of us went into her room and stood at the foot of her bed like a solemn, little army. I don't even remember who spoke the actual words to tell her about her condition. I do know that my sister told her about her options for chemo and radiation. Our mother listened to us, took a slow, deep breath and then stunned us with her quiet refusal. "Oh no," she said. "There won't be any chemo or radiation. It's time to die."

As I write this now, it seems to me that someone hit the fast-forward play button after that. I honestly don't remember the details of the next few days. We all had our reactions, of course: I have a fuzzy memory of one of trying to talk her out of dying—which seems ludicrous to me now; Julie kept giving her oncology options hoping something might inspire her to "fight it" and Tory went about preparing to have her released from the hospital. I felt as if life had slapped me awake. I was very clear about not wanting to cry. I wanted to face this moment with as much clarity as I could muster. I remember thinking "this is the real thing." Life with our mother had taught us that when she made up her mind about something that was it! She didn't want to go home. Tory suggested that we take her to his house in Mission Bay. No one had any strength to argue that it was too much for Tory to take on. We all just wanted to get her out of the hospital. Another day or so passed, and we had her comfortably installed in Tory's master bedroom with a garden view and all of us hovering around to make sure she was comfortable. We stayed together with our mother for four days: four days that we came to call "the love bucket," because it was if we were all soaking in a giant bucket of love. Our grandfather, Mom's father, Eli, joined the love party and we all took turns going in and out of Mom's room, talking, or not talking, holding her hand, rubbing her feet with peppermint lotion, feeding her bites of food as her appetite allowed, singing her the little songs she would request, but silently reeling in the truth of those minutes and hours. Mom was dying!

As I look back on those four days, I realize that it was my awakening to the greatest truth I would ever know. Every problem, every non-essential thought or emotion I had, disappeared in the face of loving my mother. My sister-in-law, Allisa, and I went to the market for groceries, and came home with nothing but ready-made comfort food. We didn't care about our diets, or our figures, or how many calories anything had. We shopped with a simple philosophy: "does that look good?" If the answer was yes, it went in the cart. "Does Mom like that?" Yes—it went in the cart. We didn't care what it cost. We weren't worried about money. We weren't worried about anything but getting food: Mac-n-cheese, watermelon, cookies, ice cream, deli chicken; we shopped until we found every possible comfort item in the store.

Along with the disappearance of our worries about the usual day-to-day operations, my stress about my relationship with my mother, my "Mom stuff," went away too. Before this crisis, my mother and I had practiced a kind of uncomfortable détente with each other for most of my adult life. Over the years, my mother had become a high-maintenance, hot-house flower. The tragedy she suffered at my father's early death had manifested in her in neurotic and painful ways. She married many times, looking for that lost love. She grew more and more self-centered, and lost the sense of humor I had loved when I was a little girl. I grew up taking care of her, hurrying home from school to "check in," sitting on the foot of her bed giving her the blow-by-blow of my day. She wanted every detail. She wanted to live my life for me. She spent hours counseling me on how to interact with my friends, who I should date, and what I should do upon graduation. I dreaded those daily sessions where she took credit for all of my achievements and disavowed knowing me when I failed. In later years, that habit morphed into actual encouragement to fail. It was as if she wanted to compete with me, to prove that she was better than me and that she could win. As I struggled to finish my PhD, I would call her from time-to-time for an encouraging word to help me keep going. I learned early in my graduate work that she wasn't available for that. On the contrary, my goal exceeded her own success, so it felt like she was actually hoping I would fail. She would encourage me to give up my dream—to walk away from it. She would tell me that I wasn't pursuing a "real" PhD, anyway and that mine was one of the "easy ones." Despite all her "encouragement" to give up my dream of completing my PhD, I finished and faced the prospect of her resentment of me, but, true to form, she took credit for me instead: taking her pride of her daughter to new heights by bragging at my graduation party, introducing herself as the "mother of the doctor" and telling everyone how intellectual our family had always been and how she was certain she had planted to right seeds in me to earn a PhD. Even though I had moved 1000 miles north from San Diego to Seattle, she still found ways to insinuate herself into the day-to-day schedule of my life with phone calls, check-ins and "news." I resented her meddling and saw her desire for extra closeness as smothering. I often felt as if my mother was like a piece of cling film that covered me, choking me and cutting off my air supply.

During the four days of our love fest, however, all of these feelings went away. It was as if I set down a heavy bag of old stories and just walked away from it, unwilling to return to reclaim my lost luggage. I had been telling myself those old stories about the "crimes" my mother had committed and holding her secretly accountable for the "damage" it caused me. My feelings of being "wronged" by my mother gave way to feelings of admiration and respect for her courage. My mother chose to make her death another one of her explorations. She had sampled many religious beliefs during her lifetime, but had not settled on one philosophy. She deeply believed that she would have a life after her death, but didn't know what it would look like. Her honesty and courage to pass through the stargate of her own beliefs was both inspiring and unsettling at the same time. Inspiring because she had found her own truths, and unsettling because the woman I saw dying did not match the woman I had called "mother" for all those years. In the face of all that love and courage, all my old stories grew still.

On the fourth day of our love fest, our Mother stunned us again by asking to get up and play the piano. She had been a concert pianist as a young girl, and though we had music in our home during my childhood, I hadn't heard her play the piano for decades. We stood around her as she began to play, slowly at first, then as she gathered strength she played as if she had never stopped playing. We all stood there, tears pouring down our faces, listening to our mother play her beloved piano one last time. "Here's one for Laurel," she said, smiling. Bumble Boogie came bounding out of the keys and we all laughed. As a child, I used to jump around the living room dancing wildly to that tune. We were all laughing hysterically by the time she finished. Then she went back to bed. When I went into her room to say good bye that evening, I couldn't bring myself to say those words. For some reason they didn't seem quite right, so instead I kissed her and said, "I love you forever, Mommy!" She smiled and answered, "Yep! That's the way it works."

A week later, Tory called. "Mom is gone," Tory said. "She wanted to go to the hospice late last night, so we called the ambulance. She died on the gurney before they could even put her into her room." It was as if she didn't want to die at Tory's house, but she didn't want to stay at the hospice, either. She was 64. The family gathered in San Diego again a few weeks later to scatter her ashes off the coast. We were all there with our laughter and tears, poetry and pictures and our love. We said our good-byes, hugged each other and went back to our lives to face the future of life without our mom.

I spent that summer processing my loss like a survivor of a tsunami. I felt as if my world had been remodeled, scrubbed clean by a huge wall of tears that ravaged my shore. As the waters receded and the wave pulled back, I began to find treasures in myself that the destruction and loss had left behind. My experience of awakening stayed with me as I remembered all the love

I felt for my mother. I had discovered a whole new set of tools to process my "Mom stuff" and while my healing was not instantaneous, it was steady and sure. The love I had re-discovered during those four days guided me through my own sorting process. I was examining the old hurtful stories with the new eyes of love, and seeing in them simple truths about my mother as a fallible woman, and myself as a child who needed healing. My personal truths were starting to emerge. For me, my mother's death had become a gateway to love, healing and the fiery testing of my most durable beliefs.

Death as an Invitation

It may sound harsh, but we are all going to die. Death is physical reality knocking on the door. It is a truth we must all face. Death tests our deepest beliefs about who we are and why we are here. Death offers us the chance to awaken, to face the unhealed pain of our old stories, to heal them and to return to the loving truth of our most essential nature. Death reminds us that our time here is limited and invites us to live more fully. It can be a door opening to a truer life: a life we must not wait to start living. It is the most profound experience any of us will have. It signals the final shift away from the integration of our physical world towards the purely spiritual aspects of our Truest Self. The internal and external aspects of our physical life give way to our eternal life as we return to spirit. Quite often as a part of that shift, our stories become dislodged, and no longer able to serve us in our final moments. They are no longer relevant in the face of this truest moment of our lives.

This is the invitation: to notice the story as separate from our True Self. This is the invitation: to shift the focus of your attention away from your view screen to your own Awareness. What could be more profound than to face the inevitability of your own death? What is a truer way to determine what you really care about, what you value and what you hold dear? If you have experienced the loss of a loved one, you already know the lessons of love available to you in that experience, but have you transformed that experience into durable beliefs for yourself? How can you redeem the pain of death with learning? Your beliefs about your life, your love and the very essence of your being are all tested in these painful moments, and you stand in the middle of an opportunity to know who you truly are and what you truly believe.

Durable Beliefs

I have had many clients confess that their beliefs had "abandoned them" in their moments of crisis. Many admit to feeling embarrassed about this, as if they have somehow failed a test. I try to encourage them by pointing out that they haven't failed: their beliefs have failed. What does that mean? It means that the belief was flawed, unable to stand the test of real life events. I call this proof that the belief was not "durable." A durable belief is a lasting and stable belief that can stand the wear and tear of your daily life. This is where the rubber meets the road—as they say. It is why people jettison their old ways of thinking when they discover they have cancer or some other life-threatening illness. Their old belief systems are not durable—they will not be able to stand up under the load of this new circumstance. In this way, death offers an invitation to "true up" our deepest beliefs: to make sure they will support us through life's most difficult challenges.

When I discuss durable beliefs with my clients, I encourage them to test their stories about what they believe against the reality of their lives. Different from the stories we tell about our beliefs, a durable belief is something more consciously derived, more practiced with experience and longer-lasting. I ask my clients to test the stories of their beliefs in much the same way manufacturers test their products. We can borrow the method and scrutiny of durability testing as a means of "truing up" our beliefs to assure that they are, in fact, durable: that they can sustain us in our moments of greatest need. The story of the belief may not hold up under the weight of the test, and when the story fails it can give them an opportunity to create a stronger, more durable belief.

In manufacturing, durability testing is designed to determine the strength of a system under load conditions, over time. It is the test of whether or not something is capable of withstanding wear and tear or decay and that it is able to perform successfully while avoiding injuries. It is lasting and stable. It is not depleted or consumed by use. Durability testing is used to prove the lasting benefits and strength of a system or product. We can use the same testing strategy with our own beliefs to ensure that those beliefs will stand up under the "load" of life and the pressure of unforeseen events.

Tool: Durability Testing

Exercise: You can use the following questions to test your beliefs. First, write down one of your beliefs about yourself, your life or your faith.

Example: My belief: I am Pure Awareness manifesting love.

Does this belief remain true under any circumstance?

Yes. Throughout my life, I have had many opportunities to test the truth of this belief, and have never experienced a condition or circumstance under which my belief fails. It has remained the truest thing I know above all other truths.

Does this belief remain whole and intact under any circumstance?

Yes. I have had my moments of despair and discouragement, but my belief in my own Pure Awareness as love has always been the source of greatest comfort and solace for me. It shows no signs of wear or decay through my use of it.

Does this belief stand the test of comparison to other beliefs?

Yes. Despite my thorough examination of many other belief systems and philosophies, I have discovered no circumstance or situation in which another belief has proven more reliable or durable than my belief in my inherent loving awareness. I have learned no fact that controverts this for me, though I have seen many scientific studies which support the notion of loving energy as a force.

Does this belief stand the test of time and help me to overcome injury, pain and hardship?

Yes. My belief in my loving awareness has sustained me my entire life and has helped me overcome many injuries, painful experiences and hardships. It has comforted me in moments of the death of loved ones, in moments of great fear and scarcity, and has helped to keep me stay calm in the face of great danger. In fact, it has done more than sustain me; it has inspired me to attempt other seemingly impossible achievements and encourages me to try other new goals.

Does this belief remain abundant and reliable even through my use of it?

Yes. In fact, my belief in my pure awareness has grown stronger and more abundant through my use of it. I now see it as a way of life for myself and as a source of love and hope for others.

This is an example of the kind of scrutiny you can perform with your own beliefs. Could your beliefs stand up to these questions? What might you discover about your beliefs by using this test to check their durability?

Durability Testing in Action

One of my clients (we'll call her Sarah) came to me when she was first diagnosed with breast cancer. Though she deeply believed that she was a spiritual being at her core, she also believed that physical illness in any body was a manifestation of some "dis-ease" in their life. She sat on my coach weeping and trying to understand why she had manifested cancer in her own body. "What is the 'dis-ease' in my life that has caused me to give myself cancer? I take good care of myself. I exercise regularly. I eat healthy foods. I don't drink. I don't smoke. How could I, of all people, let cancer into my body?" she asked me. I was full of compassion for her as she wrestled with the story of her own beliefs in this moment of personal crisis. I suggested that she use the Durability Test to check her belief story: the belief that she had manifested her own illness. She came back two weeks later after working on the test with the realization that her story was inadequate to explain the complexity of breast cancer. She realized that there were many other plausible explanations for why she had developed cancer. She had done some additional research and reading on the topic and realized that environmental pollution alone was a factor she had not considered in her original belief system. Her original belief had failed on question

#3: it had been bested by the studies showing pollution as a major contributing factor to developing many cancers—not just breast cancer. Her original belief that she had manifested her own illness could not stand up against the careful scrutiny of the Durability Test.

We worked together in the following months to develop a new belief that was far more durable than her earlier one. Sarah came to believe that maintaining her physical wellness was an important part of maintaining the quality of her life. She now believes that her physical wellness played a vital role in her victory over her cancer, and that had she been in poorer health, she may not have defeated cancer at all. She no longer believes that she caused her own illness. Instead, she believes that she can improve her ability to heal in the future by mindfully integrating her emotional, mental and physical health day-to-day. Sarah is now living a happier life with more durable beliefs to sustain her through the coming years. She continues to take good care of her physical body as a part of her new, more durable belief system.

I am not here to judge whether your beliefs are right or wrong. Who am I to say that? I am merely asking questions about their durability. Do your beliefs sustain and comfort you in the face of crisis and pain? Do they grow stronger through use – or weaker and more uncertain? Do they fail you in your hour of need? I have seen too many people's beliefs crumple under the weight of life's hardships to doubt the importance and necessity of having a durable belief system.

Tool: Building Durable Beliefs

How do you begin to create your own durable beliefs? What ingredients do you blend to build a satisfying and still practical system by which you can live? I cannot tell you what your beliefs should be, but I can tell you some true elements that will you help build sustainable, durable beliefs; beliefs that will stand the "load test" of your daily life.

1. Pragmatic: the belief must work. It must be practical, able to be implemented into a daily routine, pattern and system. The belief that you cannot be happy until you win the Lottery, for example, is not pragmatic. It is not something that you could implement on a daily basis. It gives you no happiness in the present circumstances. It holds your happiness hostage until the ransom of the Lottery win has been paid.

2. Inclusive: the belief must be good for all. Remember the moral imperative: we must consider promoting and protecting the greatest depth to the greatest span. You cannot choose to build a belief based on your own

exclusive gain, if you want to build one which is durable. It must promote the greatest good. For example, the belief that you are more important, more worthy or more special than anyone else will not support you as you face the hardships of life.

3. Expansive: the belief must create a feeling of release in you. It must leave you open and relaxed when you use it, rather than feeling fearful, guilty and uptight. Remembering your beliefs must be a source of peace and comfort to you, rather than constriction and pain. The belief that change is part of life, for example, brings openness to the idea. It is relaxing to remember it. It releases judgment and doubt as you say it.

4. Love-Based: the belief must be based on love rather than on fear. It must be grounded in the true experience of our spiritual selves in order to have the power of durability. Too many belief systems are based in fear and exclusion. They create communities of superiority: communities of "us and them." They can leave you feeling troubled, guilty and doubtful about who you truly are. You know you are on the right track with your belief-building when you can feel the sweet release and warm comfort of love embedded in your beliefs. Love is abundant; love is the source. It is the limitless expanse of creation you connect to whenever you quiet your stories and turn off your view screens.

What are your durable beliefs? Try creating a belief for yourself with those four guidelines in place, and you will be delighted with your results. You will find greater peace and solace in the face of life's hardships, and greater joy in your day-to-day life.

My Durable Beliefs

As an example, here is a short life of some of my most Durable Beliefs. I find it helpful to use them to answer the questions which seem to arise in all of us:

Question #1: Who am I?

Answer: I am Pure Awareness manifesting love.

Question #2: Why am I here?

I am here to practice loving and being loved in all circumstances.

Question #3: What is Death?

Death is the end of my physical experience here. It is also the proof that I am Pure Awareness.

Question #4: Why is there so much pain in the world?

When I separate myself from my own Pure Awareness, I become distracted by the stories I tell and the stories of the world: fear, anger, scarcity are all examples of this.

Question #5: How do I know what is True?

I know what is true when I feel love, joy and laughter. Even during times of grief, I can still feel the love that remains eternal.

You can use these questions to find your most Durable Beliefs, too.

Death as an Invitation to Heal

What works for some, may not work for another. That is why it is so important for each of us to identify our own Durable Beliefs. One of my neighbors passed away last year. Prudence was 94. She had lived a long and happy life, devoted to her church and to her belief in everlasting life. Sadly, during her final weeks, she was gripped with fear. She could find no comfort in the beliefs that had sustained her throughout her life. Her fear of death and judgment had more power over her than her life-long beliefs of salvation and redemption. Even as her family gathered around her, trying to reassure and comfort her, she thrashed in the fear of her final judgment. She accused herself of not being good enough, and had profound doubts about what her everlasting life would look like. It was as if her deeper fears, old unhealed stories, had taken the place of her beliefs.

I visited her in the Hospice and comforted her as best I could. I tried to help her heal some of her pain, but her fear had taken control of her. Unresolved conflicts and old stories have a way of re-asserting themselves into our moments before death. We die as we have lived, healed and whole or gripped in the fear generated by the old "stuff"—the old stories. Unless we consciously work to heal our old stories of fear and pain, they can re-appear in our moments of deepest crisis.

What is your "stuff"? What stories are you telling yourself that keep you isolated and distant from your loved ones? Are they "Mom stories" or "Dad stories" or something else? What are the old memories you replay on your view screen? How much pain do you keep alive in yourself, fanning the flames of old wrongs and atrocities committed against you? How are those old stories keeping you from healing? How would your life change if you could end them?

Our Stories Point the Way

I have met many clients for whom the death of a loved one was not the release from the story-telling, but rather the reinforcement of it, and others for whom the death of a parent was retribution. Sadly, some of your old stories may be true stories of pain and abuse and even criminal wrongs perpetrated against you. This does not mean that you cannot heal them, heal yourself and find a truer sense of yourself. The abuses and wrongs you might have suffered do not define you any more than they hurt you in an irreparable way. As long as you live, you have the opportunity to heal.

One of my first clients came to me just after her father had died. For Sally, her father's death was the final act of justice for a man she despised. It was the release from a curse that had haunted her for years. Sally was a model of achievement. She was beautiful, accomplished and successful in her work. After her father's death, however, she found herself plagued by bad dreams, sleeplessness and unable to concentrate at work. She had visited many therapists, participated in support groups and retreat weekends devoted to healing, but for some reason she wasn't able to let go of the old hurt. She hadn't seen her father since she left home to attend college 15 years earlier. I asked her to tell me a story about her Dad. "I never called him that!" She snapped at me. "He wasn't a Dad—he was a monster!" She went on to tell me about his repeated sexual abuse of her from the age of 13 through high school. Going to college out of state was her only escape. She suspected that her mother knew about the abuse, but did nothing to stop it. She chose not to attend his funeral even though her mother was scandalized. "I feel so angry at my mother," she admitted. "I am angrier now, than I was when I left home 15 years ago! I thought I had healed all this, but I want to go home and slap my mother's face!" After an hour of listening to those old, painful stories, I asked her to go home and write down all the stories around her abuse as if she was writing a screenplay. I asked her to write them like a novel, to remove herself from the story and tell it from the omniscient point of view, the all-knowing, observer view. She came back to her appointment two weeks later with 50 pages! She had written the script of a play in which the young girl confronted her mother, called the police on her father and left home to live in a loving friend's house. She had let herself imagine what her life might be like if she could re-create that part of her past—if she could just re-write it. We worked together for six months, while she wrote and re-wrote all the old stories of her life. It didn't change the fact that she had been abused—that could never change. It changed her way of engaging the pain. It gave her a way to release her pain through creatively imagining a different life. As she did this, she began putting herself in the role of the loving mother or her own inner child. She began loving herself as if she was her own child. She let her pain die, and in its place she found self-love. This act of love: self-love helped her heal her old stories. She loved radically on her own behalf, changing her story to protect her inner child from any further atrocities which might come her way. Her father's death was the invitation to heal her past. Whether or not she loved him, she was able to love herself and heal her old stories.

Your stories are important archives of your past, your culture and your sense of yourself, but not ALL of yourself. Stories are powerful engines for creating your present and future. When I ask you to examine your stories, I am asking you to look for clues of hurts that need healing. Your stories can point the way out of a painful past. They can point the way out of your own sense of self-doubt and limitation. If you see everything through the eyes of an old story, you will never see the situation as it is, nor will you have access to something beyond the story. You lose access to the love inside you waiting to heal your pain. The truth is that we cannot know why these horrors happen. Perhaps it is karma, pure evil, ego gone crazy and human dysfunction: these are all beliefs circling around us from various healing genres. Perhaps they all have merit, but what good are those beliefs if they do not release you from your pain? Once the atrocity has happened, all you can do is to try to learn and heal. The only true redemption that comes from any horror is the learning you can take from it and the return to loving yourself as a spiritual being. Grieving must end at some point, and be replaced with love: self-love, spiritual love.

More Love

How does a True Self experience death? In the days and weeks that followed my mother's death, I tried more and more ways to maintain my "wakefulness" in the world. I looked for ways to bring more of it into my daily life. I asked myself: "what is the most loving thing I can do in this moment?" I still struggled at work. I had employee issues and product issues. I had tough meetings with Microsoft executives. At home, I still struggled with raising my teenage son alone. I questioned my parenting: whether I was spending enough time with him, or giving him appropriate discipline, but I was trying to shift the basis of all my decisions to love. I thought about what I could do in each moment to bring more love into the situation. Though I know I wasn't perfect in any one of those situations, I also know that I always chose on behalf of love. It was my new fledgling belief that grew into the durable beliefs I have today. I am Pure Awareness manifesting love. Love is the reason we are here. Anything else is a waste of spirit.

Later in the summer after my mother died, I was having a garage sale in my new home. It was a hot, August morning and I was just putting out the sign on the curb, when a tall, handsome man rode his bicycle into my garage. I looked at him, but went about the business of selling CD's and books. After a few minutes, he called across the garage to ask about the price of the home stereo system I was selling. I walked over to him and looked into his eyes. I felt an electrical current flash through me. I think I answered his questions, but all I remember was the feeling of butterflies I had in my stomach and the electricity that continued to course through my veins.

We talked for three hours that morning. His name was Dan Ross and by the time he left to go get his truck to pick up his new home stereo system, I knew he was the one for me. He was the reason people talk about destiny and soul mates. Meeting him was the answer to the question my mother's death had posed for me: is life really all about love? Yes! Finding Dan the summer following the loss of my Mother was no accident. Her death had opened my heart in a way that allowed me to hold the love that Dan would bring into my life. Though we didn't actually "get together" until the following year, I knew that any other man would be irrelevant.

The love between us was obvious and undeniable from the first day we met. This is the story we tell about the day we met, but it is also the truth.

These are the tools of the True Self: a set of Durable Beliefs, a daily practice of healing the old, painful stories and connecting with the source of love which lives in your own Pure Awareness: the quiet center, beyond your view screens and story-telling. Find the most loving thing you can do in this moment. Quiet your fears, turn off your stories, heal your pain and manifest the truest things you know. Let your Awareness join with others, to create a world filled with love, happiness and satisfaction. Consciously write the new story of the truth you are living. Your imagination and desire can point the way, when you listen to their quiet voices.

Your Choice: Old or New?

We are all telling stories. Will you continue to tell the old stories of pain and wrongs done to you? Or will you choose to live a truer life? Write new stories that help you live a joyful, satisfied life. Let your true stories comfort you in your times of hardship. Let them help you build durable beliefs that will allow you to see the miracle you are living here. I choose love as the basis for my durable beliefs and as the foundation for all of the truest things I know. I have seen the radical changes my clients have made in their lives as they recognized their own radiant Awareness within, and I cannot help but encourage you to do the same. Henry David Thoreau said "I do not wish to come to the end of my life only to discover I have not lived." You will know you are living your truest life by the joy you feel in living it. Do not wait until the end of your life to begin. Let the inevitability of your own death be the invitation to shift your attention to love. If death is the end of the physical: the move away from internal and external to eternal, then let us face that inevitable move with love and peace rather than with fear. If death is another awakening to the light on the other side, then let that light be the Pure Awareness that carries you through the stargate into eternity. I will meet you there with my love!

CHAPTER 5

You Can't Get in Trouble for Being Yourself

In the years following my mother's death, I continued to process my "Mom Stuff." Some of the old hurts had vanished during the days before her death, but a few still had painful juice in them. While I was still a young girl, my mother began a habit of shooting barbed comments at my sister and me. Words with a sharp edge, we called them "zingers:" stinging darts of judgment wrapped in criticism with a flippant delivery. It didn't matter if they were true because they hurt. Like burrs from a weed, they would cling to our shoulders as we carried them away, only to come alive later as hurtful commentary on our inadequate lives. As adults,

Julie and I would often debrief after a visit with our mother. We would search the conversation for zingers, like we were picking off ticks from a trip into the wilderness. Sometimes they were easy to find, other times they took years to re-surface. One of those zingers came in the days when I was still married to Tony. I had come to my mother hoping for encouragement and support, wrestling with decisions about whether to go or stay and I got a zinger instead. My mother was tired of my complaining and had grown weary of the same conversation visit after visit. She was an impulsive woman, and voted her preferences by grabbing her car keys and driving away. She did not want to hear about my sad marriage anymore. She was sick of seeing my bruises: physical and emotional and grew impatient with my uncertainty. "I'm surprised you're still hanging around there, Laurel." She snapped at me. "It seems like you're getting in a lot of trouble just for being yourself!" It was a double-whammy: my mom's impatience on top of the painful decisions about leaving my marriage. It was true: I WAS getting in a lot of trouble, but I didn't have the nerve to tell her that one of the reasons I stayed was my fear of becoming like her. After five failed marriages, my mother had become a kind of anti-hero to me and I was terrified of becoming a serial monogamist. No one could accuse my mother of "hanging around" when things got tough. It seemed impossible to explain my long suffering to a woman who bolted at the first sign of trouble. My mother seemed to enjoy the zinger, too. She took to repeating it like a mantra over the years, as if she was saying it to herself.

After her death and my experience in the love bucket, the comment lost some of its sharpness and started to take on a new meaning. It became one of those zingers that continued to haunt me. It would echo across my mind in situations at work, in my parenting of Tyler and finally in my client sessions and coaching. It bugged me! Why did it keep popping into my thoughts? I had already experienced the reality of getting in trouble time and again with myself and with others just for taking a stand, or being true to myself. I had lost friends, ended relationships and argued with loved ones over being myself. In fact, I was getting in a LOT of trouble for being myself. Still, I loved the idea that percolated behind the comment. I loved the subtle promise of freedom: the release from pleasing people in favor of having a life which I lived on my own terms. Her words seemed to be giving me license to just walk away from something that didn't feel right. I worried about what people might think of me if I did that, and how they might scorn me if I didn't join in. It seemed harsh to me: almost radical when she said it, but as the years passed, and I found more of my truest self, I began to see a kind of wacky wisdom in the idea: "you can't get in trouble for being yourself, Laurel."

My answer crystallized into perfect clarity quite suddenly and unexpectedly a year or so after my mother's death. During an Appreciative Inquiry workshop I attended in Seattle, we were discussing the power we lose when we avoid taking responsibility for the things we care about. I suddenly heard my mother's zinger repeating across my mind. I realized that when I am taking responsibility for the things I care about, I am also living in alignment with my Truest Self; I CANNOT get in trouble. When I am aligned with my own highest good and making conscious, deliberate choices that reflect my loving nature, "trouble" does not exist. Though others may criticize and judge me, they do not define the truth of my actions. If someone misunderstands me, I can do what I can to explain, but, the truth is, I'm not in control of how other people feel, and their reactions and judgments are NOT my responsibility. If I have done all that I can do to "true-up" my own actions with my highest good, then any resulting reaction/response from others is their responsibility. You can't get in trouble for being yourself when you ARE being your SELF—your Truest Self. What would "trouble" even look like from that place of alignment and peace? How could anyone ever "get in trouble for being themselves?"

Getting in Trouble

It is natural to want to get along with others. Humans are innately social beings. We like to have friends, belong to a community, feel like we are a part of a system and above all we have a deep yearning to be loved. The friction begins when we take our individual "self" into that community and change or distort who we are in order to placate or please others. We learn very early what gets us in trouble. We learn what trouble looks like and how to avoid it. When a child spills a glass of milk, how often do we hear them say: "my bad!" they have already learned NOT to take responsibility for their actions because they have already learned to fear it. When fear is in the driver's seat everything we encounter can look like trouble—whether it is or not. Physically, trouble might look like being hungry, or homeless, or being in physical danger of injury or pain. Once the basics, food, shelter and safety, are in place, however, the trouble doesn't stop. Getting in trouble becomes making a mistake, being misunderstood and criticized, not being liked or feeling unloved. Trouble equals pain, isolation and punishment. I don't have to tell you what your version of trouble might be. As soon as I say the word "trouble," you immediately begin running stories and pictures on your personal view screens that tell you what your particular brand of trouble looks like.

Even when you are alone, the trouble doesn't stop. Being alone is no guarantee that you will escape the criticism, punishment and blame that accompanies trouble. Indeed, being alone might trigger more trouble about being unloved, unworthy and unpopular. We all have an internal dialogue that keeps us "in line." We all have an Inner Critic standing by to point out our mistakes and short-comings. What does your Inner Critic sound like? How much trouble do you get into after work or a lunch with friends, or after a family dinner? Do you ever beat yourself up for something you said (or didn't say)? Do you ever correct yourself, or go back over the conversation with a fine-tooth comb judging everything you said? We begin getting in trouble with ourselves long before we get into trouble in our community. In fact, your internal dialogue may even help determine how you interact with the community. Your Inner Critic may be an expert on what to say, how to lie and please people "out there." What is the answer, then? How do we stop getting in trouble for being ourselves?

"I can't win!" a client, Annie, wailed to me one afternoon. "No matter what I do, it feels like I am always getting in trouble!" She was echoing a sentiment I have heard many times before, the feeling of being trapped on a hamster wheel. "I want to spend time with my children, but we have a mortgage to pay every month. My husband complains that I don't spend enough time with him; my children complain that I don't cook dinner for them every night, and my boss complains when I'm late to work! I feel like I am a victim of my own life!" Of course she wanted to spend more time with her children, cook them dinner, cuddle with her husband and please her boss, but she was at a complete loss about how to do it all.

Your Total Cost of Responsibility (TCR)

In business, we have a term to describe the calculation we make when we are assessing the cost of doing business. It is called TCO, the total cost of ownership. In my work, I have a similar calculation for my clients. I call it TCR, the total cost of responsibility. Like calculating a TCO, calculating your personal TCR is the process of assessing the direct and indirect costs and benefits related to taking responsibility for living your dreams. The intention is to consciously determine your commitment to living your dreams based on what you are willing to change in yourself to achieve it, all things considered. In other words, how much responsibility are you willing to take to assure the outcome? It is the calculation of the behaviors and habits you will give up, contrasted by what you will gain in terms of living the life of your dreams? In business, those calculations are numerical. In my work, the calculations are integral: mental, emotional, physical and spiritual. I frequently begin my long-term coaching with clients by asking them "what are you willing to change in yourself to achieve your dreams?" We look to their costs and benefits from an Internal, External and Eternal perspective.

I Like to Sing

From the time I could talk, I started singing. I used to wander around humming little tunes to myself, singing to my dolls and singing to my family. On some days, I only sang. I sang questions to my mother and I sang conversations with my sister. You could say that singing was just who I was—it was a part of me. As I grew up, I learned very quickly, when it was ok to sing and when it wasn't. It was ok to sing in my bedroom, playing with my friends, but it wasn't ok to sing at the dinner table. In my teenage years, it was ok to sing while I was surfing: sitting on my board waiting for a fresh set of waves. It was ok to sing while I washed the dishes, or scrubbed the bathrooms. It wasn't ok to sing in the library; (I tested that one)! I learned when singing would get me in trouble and when it wouldn't. I learned to sing softly in certain situations, and loudly in others. It was ok to sing loudly in the car and ok to sing softly in the grocery store. I adapted my choices to support my love of singing. I avoided getting in trouble for singing— for being myself—by learning the social code of my community. Even as it changed, I found that I could adapt appropriately to avoid getting in trouble. I was taking responsibility for my own choice. Without knowing it, I had calculated my TCR for singing. I knew the costs and the benefits and adapted my behavior to accommodate both. Singing was an easy choice to make. I knew I loved it. I had no worry or fretfulness about whether or not it was right or wrong. My TCR became a calculation of knowing when I could sing without disturbing the community. Without realizing it, I was already practicing the necessary skills for what I would later come to call the True Self.

Tool: Calculating Your TCR

What value would you place on the peace and freedom of being your truest self in the world? What is your total cost of taking responsibility for of the things you care about? What do you have to give up to gain greater happiness? These are some of the questions you might ask yourself as you begin to calculate your own TCR. While some of your costs will be unique to you, others are universal. What follows is a brief description of those universal costs and benefits from the internal, external and eternal perspectives of my work.

Internal:

Internal Cost #1: Give up your Inner Critic. Give up your need to feel bad about yourself. This is the voice in your head with the endless litany of negative self-talk. The Inner Critic keeps you in fear, cowering in the face of the terrible things awaiting you. You cannot negotiate with your Inner Critic. You cannot talk it out of criticizing you. It was built to scare you and to keep you small. It is the servant of your story-telling, and disinterested in being "healed." It may sound silly to suggest giving it up. Why would you want to keep it? In truth, however, most of my clients resist this. They have learned to anchor their behavior in self-criticism and are often addicted to the negative "juice" it sends through their system. They love the feeling of being a victim. "I feel like I'm a victim to my own Inner Critic," Annie admitted to me, as we discussed her feelings of overwhelm. "I am afraid of being in trouble all the time—with MYSELF." Annie deeply believed that her Inner Critic was the Boss of her. "There's nothing I can I do!"she lamented to me on many occasions. Her Inner Critic was filling her view screen with self-defeating stories of powerlessness, lack of responsibility and inability to effectively change anything about her life. Her Inner Critic was one of the ways she allowed herself to feel victimized by her circumstances. As long as she was powerless, and believing her own negative self-talk, she had no responsibility to change. We spent some time unpacking all the assumptions she had piled into that self-criticism and excavating the truth of her behavior. "I guess I have always felt like I didn't really have a choice," she said with a sigh. "I never realized that I had made my choice unconsciously. I had followed the programming of my story instead of following my heart." Once Annie realized that she was making her own choice: consciously or unconsciously, she decided to make all her choices as consciously as she could. She still chose to keep her job, her family and her husband, but by making those choices consciously, she unplugged the power of her Inner Critic. She started noticing the times when her Inner Critic would kick up, and began changing her story. She became aware of her choices moment to moment and started letting her Awareness inform her decision-making. She replaced the "voice in her head," with the simple question from her Awareness: "what can I do in this moment to bring my truest values to life?" In doing so, she calculated her own TCR: giving up her Inner Critic and gaining the power of conscious choices from her own Awareness.

Internal Benefit #1: Embrace the deep wisdom of your own Awareness: your Truest Self, and allow that wise voice in your head to grow. Let your self-talk become positive and self-affirming. To do this, you must catch yourself in the moment when the Inner Critic is at its strongest and change the channel; cut off the voice stream; end the criticism. This requires patience, practice and repetition, but it is possible. Change the words from negative comments to helpful ones.

Example:

Inner Critic . . . becomes Inner Wisdom

"I'm SUCH an idiot!"

"I'm so stupid, dumb, silly . . .<insert your adjective here>" "I want to handle that situation differently the next time." (Being specific about the changes adds energy to the idea).

"I have more to learn on this subject."

I can't –

   lose weight!

   get this right!

   figure this out!

"I need to give myself more time and practice to achieve this goal. What else can I bring to this goal to help me achieve it?"

I won't give up on myself!

"I hate myself when I am like this."

"I can love myself even in the face of difficulty."

"There's nothing I can do about this."

"I have not yet discovered a solution to this."

Research shows that by finding ways to improve your internal dialogue, you increase your chances of success ten-fold. Negative self-talk is the number one contributor to failure. By embracing the wisdom of your True Self, you can silence the Inner Critic forever. Annie catches herself "in the act" of negative self-talk more and more often these days and unplugs the story-telling that goes with it. She enjoys the peace of knowing that she is consciously choosing to live a busy life. Interestingly, as soon as she took conscious responsibility for her life, her life changed. She stopped telling herself a story of being a victim of her own life, and started writing a new story of responsibility and awareness. She found solutions for spending more time with her family, making dinners and looking for romantic get-away time with her husband. She stopped being late to work, and received a promotion six months later. The first thing she changed was accepting her own responsibility for creating a happy life and in doing so found great success and joy.

Internal Cost #2: Give up the Story-telling. Give up your need to use your old stories as your reference point for seeing the world. When you tell an old story about a negative event in your life, you are letting your past define your future. It is the process of doing the same thing over and over again and expecting a different result: the definition of insanity. While we can use our stories in positive ways, this tendency focuses on all the failures and mistakes you have made in your past, telling you that you are doomed to repeat them. With this as the internal landscape, how could anyone achieve success?

A young woman named Wenda came to see me as a part of her ongoing professional development work. We soon discovered, however, that what she really cared about was having a baby. She and her husband had tried without success for two years, and she was ready to give up. "My mother was right!" She told me. "She's been warning me all along not to get my hopes up, but we wanted a baby so much that we just didn't want to believe she might be right." As I interviewed her, she told me her tragic story: she had been molested and raped as a young teenager and her mother, fearing she might become pregnant, had taken her to the doctor for a prophylactic DNC. Her mother had to lie to the doctor to authorize the procedure, but she felt that she was protecting her daughter from greater harm. Sadly, the procedure had damaged her uterus, and the doctor warned her mother that Wenda might never be able to conceive. I proceeded to ask her many questions: mostly fact-based ones, about the additional testing, research and information she might have gathered to controvert this diagnosis. After all, Wenda was now 28 and the medical advice available 15 years after her injury would certainly be different. She confessed to me that she had done almost no research about her condition. She was letting the story: that she could not conceive, rule all her thinking about why she was having trouble getting pregnant. It was an easy assumption to make, based on her history, but not one that addressed the issues she could potentially be having. I asked her to see her gynecologist and tell her the story she had told me.

She came back to see me two weeks later, beaming

with excitement. She had seen her gynecologist and been referred to a fertility specialist. She and her husband were both being tested. She had already undergone an MRI examination and her uterus was normal. It turned out that the cause of her infertility (if you can call it that) was some remaining scar tissue in one of her fallopian tubes that was blocking her eggs from reaching her uterus. A simple procedure corrected the blockage, and she and her husband became pregnant and are now the happy parents of a healthy baby boy. They are considering having another child, but Wenda, now interested in her professional development, is weighing the choice carefully. Isn't that weird??" she told me, laughing in one of our sessions. "I had been so busy telling myself I couldn't conceive; it's almost like I made it true!" No, it isn't weird! It is the power of the story and the profound freedom of taking responsibility for the things you care about. Give up the old story in favor of facts, information and research. You can blend all the information you gather into a newer, truer life!

Internal Benefit #2: Embrace your ability to write a new story. Consciously create the life of your dreams. In each moment, make the choice that aligns with your highest good, your clearest thinking and your deepest desires and you will feel like a magician capable bringing loving magic into the world. I love the idea of the vision board: a collage of images all targeted at achieving a goal. All the rage a few years ago, they take the best of positive imagination and make it visual, but why not take the idea a bit further? Why not look for ways to embed actual physical changes connected to your vision? Wenda used this idea and kept a pair of baby shoes on her desk at work all the while she and husband were gathering information. She had the baby shoes with her as she went into surgery, and her husband had them at her bedside when she awoke. She kept a visual reminder of her vision for herself. Wenda's feeling of excitement about her baby's shoes gave energy to her dream of getting pregnant. This may seem like a small thing, but it can be a powerful tool to reinforce the imaginative energy of our minds by placing a physical anchor in the world.

External:

External Cost #1: Give up your need to blame others for your failures. When your Inner Critic turns its attention to the external world, it becomes the Blame Game. The object of the Blame Game is to throw away as much responsibility and power, as possible. You look for places to throw the pain of your own feelings of inadequacy, shame and guilt. Psychologists call this projecting, and rightly so. It is your story-telling turned outwards from your internal projector. In your search for innocence, you say "It's not my fault that the airport was crowded and I missed my plane." "It's not my fault that I sent the report late; I couldn't get the right numbers from So-and-so." "It's not my fault my marriage is unhappy; my husband is never home." I hear conversations in coffee shops, in line at the grocery store and always at the airport where people are complaining about all the horrible things that have been "done" to them—as if they had no part in the problem. One young woman, Sydney, came to see me after getting fired from her job. A waitress at an upscale bistro, Sydney's boss told her that she wasn't good with the customers, and that they complained about her attitude and rudeness. She sat in my office in tears, blaming her boss, her customers, the chefs at the restaurant and even the location of the restaurant for her failure. "How am I supposed to make up for the cooks in the kitchen giving me bad food?" she asked me through her tears. "It's not my fault! The restaurant is always so busy; I don't even have time to connect with the customers." She was busily casting herself in the role of Victim on the Drama Triangle. Her boss, her customers, even the cooks were all her Persecutors and she was hoping I would be her Rescuer. Instead of rescuing her, I asked her to consider the possibility that her boss was right: that she WAS unkind to her customers, and that her attitude DID need improvement.

External Benefit #1: Embrace your ability to improve any situation by learning from it. When you take responsibility for the things you care about, you stop blaming other people when something goes wrong. You stop talking about the ways you were hurt; you stop looking for ways to punish people for wounding you so deeply. You start looking for ways in which you might have behaved differently. You look for ways to true-up your values with your actions. You use the situation as an opportunity to learn, grow and manifest greater love. Sydney was shocked at my suggestion, and turned away from her opportunity to learn. She left our session in anger, and I didn't hear from her for a few months. When I did, she told me that she had lost another job and was ready to take another look at herself. She realized that she had delayed her own learning by refusing to give up her need to blame others. In her work with me, we explored the stories which kept her from taking any responsibility and she discovered the freedom and power of having "skin in the game." When you give away your responsibility by blaming others, you are also giving away ALL your power to change and improve the situation.

External Cost #2: Give up Group Story-telling. Stop joining in the "rag sessions." This is the slippery slope of engaging in negative group talk with your friends, family and colleagues. It is responding to the same impulse you feel internally, but now it turns outward to find power from the group. "Misery loves company"— is the old saying, and it is never truer than during the group story-telling in which you engage. It is the proliferation of negativity. It creates cynicism amplified by the communal energy of the group. Check your own personal experience to verify this: how many times have you complained to a friend about something "done" to you only to feel the anger resurface, larger than it was in the moment. Friends, family, work colleagues all have a way of turning up the emotional volume on your victimized position. That energy keeps you frozen in complacency. As long as you share the story with friends who support your negativity, you will remain stuck in the past.

While I was in high school, my mother would often call me into her bedroom at the end of the day to tell her about my activities and school work. I sat on the foot of her bed, relating all the gossip from school, the girls who were mean, the guys who were arrogant and the teachers who were unsupportive. I poured out all the injustices that had been done to me and all the wrongs I had suffered. Night after night, we had this ritual: my mother listening while I complained. Sometimes she would egg me on. She would amplify my dissatisfaction and actually encourage me to feel bad about a situation I thought I had resolved. I often left her room feeling worse than I had before I had talked to her. I left feeling unable to solve any of the problems I faced and trapped in a world I did not understand. This feeling grew so strong that I finally decided to graduate early and leave home. I finished high school mid-term in my senior year and moved out to live with my sister and attend the local community college while I decided my next steps.

External Benefit #2: Set limits for your own behavior. Look for ways to take more responsibility for your part of the problem instead of projecting your pain outward. Use your time with friends to amplify positive changes in your life rather than celebrating your defeats or re-hashing old pains. I didn't realize it then, but by leaving the bed-time ritual behind me, I was taking responsibility for having a happier life. I gave up my group story-telling with my mother and took action to feel better. I didn't like high school, so I finished early and left. I didn't like the rag-sessions that left me feeling like a victim, so I moved away from home. My sister and I were too busy having fun to sit on each other's beds at night complaining. We practiced being happy.

When you take responsibility for surrounding yourself with activities which align with your True Self, you will change your world. While it is possible that some of your friends will not appreciate your efforts, it is comforting to know that you are giving others the chance to change. My mother was not happy, at first, when I moved away from home. In fact, you could say that I got in trouble for being myself that time—except for the fact that I knew I was doing the right thing. I was sorry that my mother chose to have her feelings hurt, but the truth was I had acted in alignment with my own highest good rather than choosing the storytelling. I chose to interrupt our habit in favor of my own values and preferences. I calculated my own TCR and decided that giving up my need to please my mother and join in our group rag sessions brought me a greater sense of happiness and integrity. Instead of sitting silently resenting the situation, I took myself out of it.

Eternal:

When you are living in alignment with your True Self you have no costs to calculate, because you cannot "get in trouble." You behave from the loving, radiant core of your individual spark of the Divine. You are "trued-up." You harm no one and no one can harm you. Perhaps you have heard the stories about the Peaceful Warrior: the man who travels the world interacting with peace and love. In one such fable, the Warrior bars the way of a thief with a knife who threatens to kill him if he will not let him into a nearby hut. The Peaceful Warrior refuses, knowing that women with babies are inside. The thief says, "I will kill you!" The Warrior replies, "then you must kill me, because I will not let you into this hut." Confounded by the quiet strength and courage of the Warrior, the thief fled. It is a fable and a metaphor for what is possible for us all. When we have the courage to stand for our convictions, the world will step aside. The Warrior was willing to die for what he cared about. Few of us are ever faced with life and death decisions like this one, but in some ways our decisions are no less powerful. For Annie, who decided to live her life with conscious choice, for Wenda who decided to take responsibility for checking the facts of her own story-telling and for Sydney who had the courage to face her part of the problem, they all changed their lives. In the "small" decisions of our lives, we define who we are. We bring the loving energy of our True Self into the world. The benefits of this are countless. They multiply everyday in direct proportion to the willingness you put forth to stay True to yourself.

Get Out of Jail Free

What else do you need to know to begin to live the life of your dreams? You must take full and complete responsibility for the things you care about. "Does it mean I get to do whatever I want to do?" a skeptical client once asked me. "What do you want to do?" I countered. Taking responsibility does not mean you have a Get out of Jail Free card in the game of Monopoly. It doesn't mean you can go out and hurt people just because you feel like it. I hope that's not what you have been thinking. It simply means that our notions of what constitutes trouble change as we align our behavior with our truest values. Taking responsibility for what you care about is simply that; it is taking full responsibility: heart, mind, body and soul, for all the love you can bring into this world in as many ways as you feel drawn to do. This is the way of the True Self: to bring your full attention into each moment with love, and begin consciously creating the life you want to live. It means taking those durable beliefs you identified for yourself in Chapter 4, and road-testing them in your day-to-day living.

When you do this you will begin to notice the change that takes place in you and in others around you. Your fear transforms. It changes from "getting in trouble" to manifesting the truth of who you are in the world. Instead of being afraid of that, you become excited and anticipate with joy what can happen next. It changes from needing to protect yourself from those "wrongs" being done to you into becoming a change agent for redeeming a negative situation. In fact, you might actually find yourself looking forward to opportunities to make this change in the world. You might look at all the daily difficulties of living as rich opportunities to manifest more love. Where you once felt the fear of scorn from others, or abandonment, you can feel the power of knowing you are a piece of the Divine. You are never alone. You are always connected by that silken cord of spirit. Mistakes become opportunities for learning and expansion, rather than events for punishment and shame.

Your Choice: Will you or won't you?

One of my favorite activities is to sit on our deck and look out at the lake below our home. On quiet nights, as I sit and reflect on the great joy available to all of us I catch myself wondering: is this work I do magic? Is it magic that allows people to change their lives? In a way, it is! It is the magic of being willing to accept the simple truth that you hold the power to live the life of your dreams. The power is in the responsibility you are willing to take for yourself and your actions. It is the power of your own integrity and the manifestation of your highest good. No one can do what you can do in the same way that you will do it. This is the magic of your individuality in this world. You are the powerful magician who can call it forth. Your loving energy can only come through you. How long will you wait to let your light shine? The world needs you and your love so desperately. You don't have to be a famous celebrity, or movie star; you don't have to be in a position of power— you are already in a position of power. You are standing in your own skin. You have all the creative energy to change your world. What is the first thing you can do in this moment? You can make the conscious choice to love. You can make all your choices consciously from this moment forth. You can awaken to the miracle of who you are! You are the only one who can!

[1] This is a sample list from one of clients written with his permission.

CONCLUSION

Start Here

As I mentioned in the Introduction, I decided to write this book because I wanted more people to know about the simple truths I have discovered during my life and work: truths which I believe will help everyone live a happier life. I didn't always know what my book would look like as I worked on it. Now, beginning this conclusion I see all the ideas I have considered over the years. I see the influences of centuries of thinking, stretching and learning. How did I know where to start? The truth is I didn't—I just started! At first I thought my book would be about radiance and then happiness, then abundance and finally I realized it would be about all of those things and more. It didn't really matter that I didn't see this book as I began this project. What mattered was starting. One step led to another and soon enough I was walking towards my goal of writing this book. Where can you begin to live the life of your dreams? You can start here in this moment, simply by placing your attention on your own Awareness: your True Self. What is the story that is active on your view screen now? Is it a story about how hard it will be to change? Is it a story about your fear of losing something: an old habit or behavior? Whatever it is, notice it. See it. There it is flashing on your view screen in front of you. If you can see it, you can also notice that it is not you. You can return your attention to your own Awareness and breathe quietly. Now, from this place of peace and quiet and gentle breathing you can ask a new question: in this moment what do I care about the most? What is the most loving thing I can do for myself? I cannot tell you what you will hear. I cannot tell you what you care about most deeply. I can tell you that your answer to those questions will lead you into your new life: the life of your dreams. It is that simple; it is that hard. Listen now from this place of gentle peace. Whatever you hear can be your first step. No doubt your first step will lead to your second step and many more as you keep returning to your own awareness: your True Self. In this way, we can begin to live a truer life in each moment. There is no journey and no destination because each moment is the point of entry.

Each moment is the first step.

My Favorite Question

I love it when people ask me: "What can I do to live a spiritual life?" I love it because it is so easy to answer. I've heard other teachers, self-help leaders, New Age spiritualists and gurus answer this question, too. Depending on their philosophy, their answers offer daily visioning practices, deep meditation, careful diet and yoga practice and prayer. All of those are lovely practices, and I appreciate the peace we can access through each of them, but it seems to me that the answer to the question "What can I do to live a spiritual life?" is "nothing." You can do nothing to live a spiritual life because you are already living a spiritual life. You have always been living a spiritual life because you are a spiritual being. We might do better to ask "what can I do to live a human life?" because that is what we are here to do. We are here to live the incalculable miracle of this physical experience. We are here to manifest the divine truth of our essential loving nature in this physical world. What can you do to live a human life? You can shift your attention away from that spiritual story which suggests that you are on a journey to enlightenment. You can ask yourself what you care most about in this moment and act in alignment with that. You can wake up to the truth that you are a being of love living a human life, a life in a body on a planet full of physical experiences and requirements.

I do not know what any of that will look like for you, specifically. That is part of the mystery of this life. We each have myriad ways to bring love into the world. That is why we have an individual presence here. That is what we are here to learn and experience: the infinite variety and diversity of expression which love can manifest. What better way to bring your joy alive than to live fully in this physical world? You do this by taking responsibility for the things YOU care about, driven by your own durable beliefs. You do this by shedding your old stories defined by fear and exclusivity. You do this by aligning your actions and goals with your own Awareness and the things your Truest Self really cares about, then work to see them realized in your life.

Though I do not know what specific miracles you will manifest for yourself, I do know that when you return your attention to your own Awareness, your life will be transformed. Your time will be filled with bringing your attention back to your True Self, creating space between that Awareness and the view screen in front of you. It will become a daily practice of identifying your true values and desires and bringing them into the world. You will find in that single move that there is so much to do day-to-day that you will have little time for unhappiness. Depression goes away. Fear becomes curiosity as you notice the stories getting triggered on your screen. Your Inner Critic loses its teeth. As you feel happier, your need to blame others and your fear of getting in trouble will vanish. You will fill your days with the joy of bringing all of your Truest Self into the world and at the end of the day and at the end of your life, you will look back knowing that you gave your life ALL of your attention and did not spend your days lost in the story of it. Everything you need to live the life of your dreams is already within you! You are already here!

Back into the Garden

It has been many years since I first held my rusty lantern above my head and looked at the quiet beauty of my dream garden. That early realization has continued to inform my practice of seeing the world without the transparent overlay of my own story. I have practiced replacing my fears with love, releasing the grip of scarcity in favor of abundance. I have practiced truing up and redeeming the pain and self-imposed suffering of my old stories. I have practiced taking responsibility for the things I care about. I have worked with many people to help them see the beauty of their own garden and find the simple truths that now author new stories of joy and abundance in their lives. I have come to see that the garden of my dream is the true world that is possible for all of us if we can stop using our old stories to define our future. The garden is your dream waiting to be realized in your own life. The garden is the perfect place to do this work. It provides us with everything we need to dislodge our stories, awaken to the truth of our eternal nature and live with love.

Are you telling yourself: "There must be something more to life than this?" Do you find yourself yearning for it: this something more? This is the call of your Truest Self, waiting for you to shift your attention away from your stories and back to the truth of who you are. Let your yearning be your reminder to breathe quietly and return your attention to your own Awareness. Let your lust, your envy, and your feelings of competitiveness draw you back to your own Awareness. Let all those negative, self-defeating stories that keep you small and contracted become reminders for the true life that is waiting for you on the other side of your view screen. You can convert every story on your screen into something positive and rich for learning when you decide to stop letting your past define your future. All the pain can be converted into learning; all the stories can be harvested for the seeds they give you to live a happier life. I take the pain of losing my sister, my mother and all the choices I have made, consciously and unconsciously, in my life as lessons to be redeemed for future happiness. I choose to grow from those lessons. What will you choose?

Your Original Contribution

"Will you or won't you have it so?" William James asked us over a century ago, and for many of us the question remains unanswered. We are here for the individual experience of our lives and his question points to the way we can live it—by choice. We have the blessing and privilege of choosing how we will manifest our individual expressions of love. Internally, externally and eternally there is much at stake. We stand on the brink of a tipping point, ready to surge forward into a world that has never been possible until now. Never before have the stakes for change been this high. Never before has the whole world faced the same set of problems. In this set of problems we have a unique opportunity to rise and implement a set of solutions driven by conscious, loving efforts. This is a unique opportunity for us all. How shall we respond to this? Will you have the courage and strength to bring your loving gifts into the world? You can keep your heart unshaken by the stories that fill your view screen. You can extricate your Self from those stories and shift your attention to your own Awareness. You can choose to live in alignment with your Truest Self. You can choose to act on behalf of your highest good. You can choose to live the life of your dreams. This is your original contribution to the world. This is what you can do in this moment and in every moment that follows, and you are the only one who can! No one else can do what you can do. That is why you are here!

How might the world be different if we all chose to make our own original contribution consciously every day? I can imagine a world where people are awake to the truth of who they are; they make their original contributions. Nothing is too small or too large. How could we say that one contribution is greater than another: growing a healthy garden, collecting the trash, piloting a jet full of people, raising a loving child, inventing a new tool to save energy, cleaning up our water and food sources? All of these contributions are determined by the passionate hearts who take responsibility for what they care about and act in alignment with their love. I can imagine a world without war, without famine; a place where our women and children are safe the world over. Though we will always have big issues and problems to solve, we can bring all of our loving radiance to the task of solving them instead of using the brokenness of our old stories heavy with the pain and politics which now defines our world. I can imagine a world where everyone uses their gifts and talents to make the world a better place. Each of us has something to give to this world, our own unique spark of the divinity we carry inside us. No one else can do this for you.

A Lovely Ride!

As a teenager in the 70's, I grew up singing James Taylor's music and learned the secret of life: "try not to try too hard; it's just a lovely ride." Despite all the hardship and pain which is inevitable in this life, your life is an absolute miracle of creative energy. That creative energy lives inside all of us! Of course, we can change our lives! Of course, we can change the world! We are the embodiment of all of that creative energy that poured into the making of this world, this universe and this moment. We are the creators of this moment and every moment that follows. What are the implications of this? What is your responsibility? Stop living your life defined by your fear; it isn't real. Stop believing that you are your story; you are not. Stop believing the story is true; it is only partially true. Begin here and now to see yourself as the radiant, loving being that came into this physical experience to manifest more love, more joy and more creativity in the world. Take the lovely ride that life offers you; relax and breathe and let your heart fill with joy and gratitude for the blessing of every moment you are given to live.

What will you do with the rest of your life? Surely, time will pass—it always does, but how will you fill those minutes? "Will you or won't you have it so?" Will you continue to live in your story, defined by self-limiting fear or will you shift your attention to your True Self and let all that creative beauty pour into this world? Find the truest things you know and bring them into the world. One truth at a time, you will change your life. The world needs your truth so desperately, and you are the only one who can give it.

. . . and in the final moments of reading this book, I send my love and best wishes to you as you begin the adventure of your lifetime!

We never know how high we are (1176)

We never know how high we are
Till we are asked to rise
And then if we are true to plan
Our statures touch the skies—

The Heroism we recite
Would be a normal thing
Did not ourselves the Cubits warp
For fear to be a King—

We never know how high we are
'Til we are asked to rise—
Then—if we be true to plan
Our statures reach the skies—
The heroism we recite
Would be a normal thing—
Did not ourselves the cubits warp
For fear to be a King—

—Emily Dickinson

CPSIA information can be obtained at www.ICGtesting.com
Printed in the USA
LVOW07s0422011214

416395LV00001B/14/P